Riding the Waves of Life

A Guide to Joyful Living

by

Kambiz Naficy

Saving Grace

Monarch butterfly
flutters
frantic
in October gales
she barely escapes
the haling leaves

Her tired wings
collapse
as she stumbles
spiraling down
to the swords
of the evergreen

For a moment it seems
all is lost

But a breath of grace
kisses her wings
as she unravels
like
the peacock fan
of a Persian king

Easing
she glides
on the homeward wind

Contents

Acknowledgements 7

Preface 8

Introduction 11

1 Living in the Present Moment 14

2 Healthy Breathing; Awareness and Control of the Breath 27

3 Meditation: Practice and Benefits 38

4 Kriya Yoga 56

5 The Quantum God 64

6 Space: The House of God 75

7 The Laws of Effortless Action in the Material World 79

8 Life as a Mirror 89

9 Relationships 92

10 Understanding Our Emotions 105

11 Money and Wealth 120

12 The *Guru*-Seeker Relationship 132

13 *Kundalini Shakti* 138

14 Ego 144

15 The Mind 151

16 The Human *Chakras* 170

17 Understanding and Managing Fear 178

18 Steps Along the Spiritual Journey 186

19 Creative Visualization 198

20 Silence   203

21 The Power of Thought   207

22 The Spiritual Laws of Nature   213

23 How to Experience Truth   223

24 Intuition   230

25 Inviting the Presence of God   239

26 Prayer   242

27 Self-Esteem   249

28 Affirmations   262

29 Developing the Courage to Change   266

30 Developing a Mind of Unlimited Potential   275

31 Compassion   283

32 Understanding and Curing Addictions   288

33 The *Guru* and Spiritual Practices (*Sadhana*)   294

34 Contemplation   298

35 Practical Application of Spiritual Principles   302

36 *Prana* and the Six Bodies   308

37 Going Beyond Our Limited Beliefs   313

38 Completion - Coming Full Circle   317

Acknowledgments

I would like to thank many of Joy of Life's colleagues and friends for making this book a reality. I extend special thanks to Sapna, Narsi, Emily Paul and Mary Picard for their patient editing work and help in the book publishing process.

Kambiz Naficy
Founder
The Joy of Life Organization

Dear Simanjit ;

Know that your life will be blessed from this meeting on

Kambiz Naficy
Feb. 1, 2015

Preface

There was a time, at the beginning of my own journey that I looked up to the experience of enlightenment as if peering at a mountain peak from the valley below. It was something to be attained by climbing the most difficult of paths. Dying and leaving the body seemed a prerequisite for making contact with the God Force.

Then, one day sitting in a bare, rented room in India, I gazed at an old radio sitting on a neighbor's shelf across the alley full of monkeys. The mason who owned the radio was fiddling with the tuner trying to tune into something uplifting. Empty-minded and unassuming, I was simply witnessing this scene when suddenly something flashed across my mind—*if you want to find God, right here, right now, all you have to do is change your frequency and tune into His channel!*

Up until then, I had spent a decade practicing Hatha Yoga, Transcendental Meditation, and Kriya Yoga. Just in the first eighteen months of my journey, I had read some three hundred books of Christian spirituality, Sufism, Vedantas, quantum physics, and energy field theory. They were all cool drinks that quenched my curiosity, but as precious as each piece of information was, the puzzle had not come together until that moment in Puttaparthi.

A voice was whispering in my mind, *Remember how radio technology works? If you can say "hello" in a radio station and increase the vibrational frequency of that word, it will travel through empty space and someone with a radio set tuned into your frequency can actually pick up your message across two continents. What if God is constantly around me, like water around a fish, what if the only problem is that I am not tuned into the divine frequencies?*

Is a fish aware of water all around it? What if God is here, all around me, and with me now? These whispers kept echoing in my mind as I walked into the Ashram and climbed up to a garden with a tree that had ribbons tied to all its branches. There was a feeling of calmness within me, as if I was walking in a cocoon of silence. I began to witness my legs moving, but the witness no longer owned the legs.

As I leaned against the old tree, the sea-like sound of silence rose to a deafening volume, and before I knew it, the garden was spinning around as if caught in a whirlwind. My spine grew very hot and I lost all body consciousness. I felt like I was vibrating at higher and higher frequencies; vibrating and dancing like the atoms beneath my molecules. For an instance there was a dreadful fear of dying, as if a life-thread was breaking. Then, the thread broke and the bright lights behind my eyelids shot out of my body and into space. The "I" was no longer solid or tied to the body, the "I" was dead and the fear was suddenly gone. The energy that was individually me was now pure, high frequency light throbbing in space.

There was only space and One primordial throb, a vibration that was not who "I" used to be. The throb or pulsation was the feeling of intense love and was very conscious, even conscious of Kambiz's body leaning uselessly against the old tree.

I now live with the realization that this light, this high frequency, primordial vibration is Infinite Intelligence that can go within itself and instantly create anything from within—even Kambiz.

I hope that by absorbing the knowledge in this book, you can tune into this divine frequency and grow into harmony with all natural forces. Once you learn the techniques described herein, you can tune into the God Channel and achieve whatever your heart desires.

Many Blessings

Introduction

The title of this book, *Riding the Waves of Life: A Guide to Joyful Living*, accurately reflects the quality of its contents, for this is not just about meditation, yoga, or spiritual practice; it is a unique composition of lessons for attaining greater joy in one's life and in this lifetime. It makes the seemingly impossible possible and lends to the human being in this material world access to her own soul. It does so through opening a window to the Self in its myriad dimensions – the psychological, emotional, spiritual, physical, and the practical. The author's point of entry for taking the seeker on this journey of understanding the Self is almost imperceptibly familiar; it is the type of life we live now in this present world. The reader will easily recognize himself or herself in the 'raw material' of the content. This is a book for the lay person with a sliding scale, equally for the individual who has never contemplated the spiritual self as for the seeker who has practiced meditation but not thought about the effects of self-limiting beliefs on his own potential.

Each lesson is a series of punctuated messages, some practical and some profound, but flowing from one to the next in a clear and accessible manner to the aspirant. The headings are guideposts that navigate the reader from one critical message or instruction to the next. Many of the messages are very brief, as they go to the very core, without adornment or justification. The words are, to the seeker, words of advice whose source is the spiritual master.

The flow of the 38 lessons has an almost poetic momentum; each one is important and can be read individually, but as you read on, the subsequent lesson deepens the meaning of the first. The lessons are a seamless weave. The reader will not notice any shift in emphasis from the spiritual self to the emotional self to the individual who plans and acts in the world, because the underlying weave blends these messages invisibly but intelligently. The whole being is brought into consideration which is essential for the lay person in learning to incorporate spiritual practices into daily life and continue living in the world. In the material world, human beings must make use of its resources, e.g., money, to fulfill their purpose and bring expression to their inner joy. So the lesson "Money" (lesson 11) transitions to a lesson on the relationship with the guru (lesson 12). These have congruence with one another because the person who trusts in the unlimited abundance of the Universe (money, being one form) is the same person whose genuine seeking brings about a Guide.

Sprinkled throughout the lessons, the author borrows from ancient scripture and physics, but purely for their relevance to understanding the Self and realizing our potential. Thus, the messages bear simple truths revealed through the power of the author's own experience and sifted from the knowledge that lies in the vast literature on the Vedas, yoga, or quantum physics.

"Simple" truths can be so simple yet so contrary to the way most people live life and the assumptions they carry around with them. For instance, *if you want to change your life, all you have to do is change your thoughts and beliefs*. This is a simple truth that can seem absurd taken in isolation, but the narrative flow brings you to a point of understanding how this can be true. Still, nothing is wholly accepted until it comes through one's own experience; to that end, the author suggests practices in each lesson to get you beyond mere knowledge.

The seeker who absorbs the messages with an open mind and applies some of the exercises to daily life will find that radical change *is* possible. Self-transformation is not a lofty goal reserved for ascetics;

it is our right as human beings and these lessons are a concrete set of steps, infused with the wisdom of a spiritual master.

Mary Picard

Lesson 1

Living in the Present Moment

The motion of the atom as it spins the fabric of life is instantaneous and unique in every moment. All of life and creation only arise in this moment; the past and the future have no place in the act of creation or living life to its fullest.

Within the present moment we experience the fullness of life as it is being created all around us. Within the present moment, we naturally feel lightness and joy associated with being in touch with life and divine creation.

What Separates Us from the Present Moment

What separates us from the joy of living in the NOW is our busy mind and our ego (the sense of "I" that feels separate from all others). The instant we are entangled with personal thoughts and emotions, we lose contact with the God Force that surrounds us in this moment.

Whenever we are thinking, we are either thinking about the past or the future; it is impossible to be engaged in thought and simultaneously be living in the present moment.

The minute we lose contact with this moment, fear and worry creep into the mind and we begin to invent problems instead of being open to solutions.

Solving the Problems of the Mind

The problems of the mind cannot be solved by the mind; as soon as you solve one problem, the mind and ego invent the next one. Herein lies the basic failure of any healing technique that seeks to work with the mind and ego in order to cure these parts of us. As Einstein believed, you cannot solve any problem from the same level at which the problem arises.

To solve the problems of mind and ego, one has to transcend the mind and the ego by slipping into the gap between two thoughts or the pause between two breaths.

I have met intellectuals who are convinced that by analyzing personal thoughts and problems they can cure their anxiety and worry. The problem with that approach is that when we follow thoughts downstream and analyze our thoughts, we actually experience more thoughts. Analyzing thoughts and becoming identified with them simply energizes more thought bubbles and takes us further away from the NOW which is free of fear and worry.

The way to be rid of fear and worry is to witness thoughts and emotions instead of identifying with them.

Witness Your Mind and Step into the Moment

To step into the moment, you need to quiet your mind by turning it inward on itself so it can witness its own chatter.

This ability cannot be taught through theory; it can only be directly experienced. I will now give you some simple instructions:

> Stare at a white wall as if you are staring at the movie screen of your mind. Begin to breathe very, very slowly. After a very deep

and slow inhalation pause your breath as you stare at the white wall. While you are breathlessly staring at the plain white, wait very intensely for the next thought to arrive. As you await the next thought, you will be surprised to find that as long as you wait for the next thought, it will never arrive! When you need to exhale, do it very slowly and imagine that any mental chatter is flowing out of your nostrils with the motion of your exhalation.

You can repeat the breathless witnessing of the mind several more times. During each round, renew your slow and deep inhalation; hold the breath while awaiting the arrival of yet another thought. Follow this silent observation period by a slow exhalation, imagining any thoughts flowing out of your mind and your nostrils during the exhalation.

Why are there no thoughts when you breathlessly await the next thought? This is because as you await the next thought, you are actually observing and witnessing your mind. The mind hates to be watched because the mind is shy and will fade if you witness it. The mind is also very stubborn and will do just the opposite of what you wish. Therefore, if you vigilantly await the next thought, the stubborn mind will do just the opposite and will not provide you with any thoughts!

That gap of thoughtlessness and breathlessness is the Void filled with lightness and joy. All creativity arises from that Void.

Accessing the Source of the Mind

The wellspring of the mind is that breathless gap between two thoughts. The mind really wants to go there because it is naturally refreshed and energized when it dips into the Void.

That thoughtless Void is also called Pure Consciousness in yogic terms. The ancient Indian scriptures (Vedantas), state that Pure

Consciousness is alive, intelligent, and buzzing with the God Force. Actually, the Vedas say that Pure Consciousness is the same as the God Force. We will explore this claim more deeply in Lesson 5 (The Quantum God).

When the mind is bathing in the emptiness of Pure Consciousness, we experience infinite creativity and divinity. This silent and breathless Void is the Source of the mind, the Source from which all thought, intelligence, and creation arises.

Problems Do Not Exist in the Present Moment

Situations that need our attention always exist, but problems are an invention of the mind and the ego. What I am saying is that difficult situations requiring your attention are real and they do exist in the present moment, but if you stay intensely present and clear minded, you will see that problems do not exist in the moment, only issues that need to be managed. Our ego/mind always dwells on the past or the future; this is where problems are invented based on fear and worry. Problems, anxiety, tension, and worry are all a product of thinking about our past or future.

Make Way for Solutions

When we quiet the mind and live in the moment, we open up mental space so that nature and the God Force can offer solutions. When our minds are full of fears and worries, we literally don't leave any room for solutions to move into our lives. Stay awake and open to what the moment brings; you will pick up on nature's clues and solutions.

When you pay intense attention to the present moment, you are honoring all of life. When you are very present, everything and everyone around you feels your deep and loving attention. Through this deep attention and compassion, you fall into harmony with the God Force and this Force will offer you all required solutions and support.

The wise person honors everything in life, yet, he is not attached to any particular outcome because such a person fully trusts the grace flowing in from the God Force. Living in the present moment, the wise one tries his best in any project, then leaves the particular results to the grace of the God Force.

Spontaneous and Right Action

Some students who are business and political leaders have asked, *How can I conduct my detailed planning and formulate future strategies if I just exist in the thoughtless moment?*

The answer is that when we are focused on the NOW, our mind is naturally clear and relaxed; our body and our breathing are also relaxed. In such a state, the mind is clear, yet very alert to the needs of the moment. When we are in tune with the needs of this moment, we can spontaneously and appropriately take care of the needs of this moment. If the present moment requires any creative thoughts and solutions, these will naturally arise from that empty space of infinite creativity — the gap between two thoughts. Here is a spiritual truth: your joyous and successful tomorrows arise from today's right thoughts, words and actions.

Enlightened people are very active; they act with clear and relaxed minds that are intuitively tuned into the needs of the moment. As they take care of the needs of today, their future automatically blossoms.

Meditation and Exercises for Living in the Present Moment

The second part of this lesson explores different meditation techniques and exercises to develop your ability to live more in the present moment. Be patient with yourself as you explore the different meditations and exercises presented here.

As you work with these exercises and other exercises presented throughout the book, you may find it useful to keep a journal. A spiritual diary can be beneficial in noting your experiences and later, as mentioned in other lessons, for documenting patterns that might provide you with further insight into your spiritual and psychological development. This journal is for your own benefit; it is not something you will share with others. Therefore, it is important to take time to establish and maintain a loving, open and honest relationship between you and your spiritual diary.

Meditation - Relaxation and Awareness of the Inner Body

Take a minute to relax your body in a lying down posture. Tense and relax all your body parts starting from the tip of your toes up to the top of your head.

Take 15 *Ujjayi* breaths into your stomach focusing on slow, smooth, long, deep, and rhythmic breaths. The *Ujjayi* breath makes a hissing sound. To practice the *Ujjayi* breath contract the glottis (a muscle in the back of the throat) as you inhale. Sense your breath almost scraping past the back of your windpipe. The *Ujjayi* breath makes a hissing sound or the sound "AH" during both inhalation and exhalation.

As you continue with *Ujjayi* breaths, tense and relax your feet, shins, thighs, buttocks, stomach, chest, shoulders, throat, and face.

Take your attention up and down the entire body. Do a body check on your entire body — toes, shins, thighs, buttocks, lower abdomen, chest, hands, arms, shoulders, throat, and face.

In your mind, visualize a scale or gauge that measures your body tension. The number 100 represents very high tension, and the number 0 represents complete relaxation. Focus on totally relaxing every part of your body while in your mind's eye you watch the tension gauge drop down toward zero (total relaxation). Once in a while during the exercise, while scanning a particular body part, stop to notice where the gauge is. Then, focus on dropping the tension levels another 10-15 points. Watch the tension gauge as you consciously relax your body, part by part.

Mindfulness Meditation on Sensations of the Inner Body

Again scan your entire body. Be aware of different qualities of physical sensations: tingling, butterflies in the stomach, aching heart, choked emotions in the throat, throbbing in the head or behind the eyes.

Take away your judgments; do not try to "figure it out". Just drop your analytical mind! Make friends with the body sensations and witness all sensations. Each time you are pulled back into the thinking process, very gently take yourself back to the feeling process within the body. If need be, bring your awareness back to your breathing from time to time.

If you feel a blockage or pain in a certain part of your body, become very aware of that body part and breathe *Ujjayi* breaths into the center of the pain or blockage. Your intention in this exercise will be to utilize gentle breathing to direct love and acceptance to that pained part.

Can you associate the physical sensation with emotions of fear, embarrassment, anger, jealousy, sadness, or frustration? What you have not accepted, what you have judged in the past, has probably now turned into a painful knot in your body cells and muscles.

See if you can identify the physical location of each emotion. Emotional energy actually moves in your body. Be aware of any physical reactions that arise out of your emotions. Just witness how emotions are impacting your physical body.

Meditation—Bringing the Five Senses to the Present Moment

Sit comfortably with your head, neck, and spine in vertical alignment. Take 15 deep, slow, long, smooth, and rhythmic breaths into your stomach. Do not breathe into your chest first; relocate your breath from your chest down to your stomach.

Hearing

Initially, close your eyes and put your focus on any sounds in or outside the room. Keep listening with greater focus and see how many different sounds you can hear.

After you are attuned to the sounds surrounding you, focus your attention on the hum or high pitched ring of pure silence (silence has a sound like the sea). As you listen to the sound of pure silence, the hum of silence will grow louder. If you cannot hear the sound of silence, you can plug your ears with your fingers. This is a meditation by itself; it will immediately quiet the mind and dissolve its chatter.

To further enhance your hearing meditation, play a beautiful piece of music and listen deeply. Feel the vibrational quality of the music in your body. Follow the sound of one instrument in this piece of music. With a little practice, you can physically feel musical notes passing through your body.

Listening

Most people listen with their mind which means they do not listen to others because the listener's mind is too busy. When you listen through your mind, you are not listening or acknowledging the other person. As part of the hearing exercise, you can work with a partner on listening. One partner will talk while the partner listening will be asked to pay deep attention:

1. First, just hear the sound of the speaker's words; do not pay attention to the words or their meaning.

2. Second, the listening partner will prepare answers or interject comments while the speaker is still speaking; here the listener is engaged is personal thinking and is still not paying much attention to the speaker.

3. Third, the listening partner will close her eyes and listen to the quality of the speaker's voice; this is a method for listening better.

4. Fourth, as the listening partner, feel the energy in your own body as you listen to the speaker. How does the speaker's energy field affect you?

5. Finally, look deeply into the eyes of the speaker and listen deeply without interruption. See if you can pick up the speaker's underlying emotions and intentions. If you remain intensely present, you will even have insights about the speaker's soul and essence as you listen to her.

Sight

Select an object like a small rock or seashell. Focus on every minute detail of this object—dimensions, color, curves, cracks, etc. Is there a part of the object that draws your attention to it? Focus on that point with a steady, unwavering gaze. Let your gaze be a soft one as you focus on that single point. What is happening to your perception?

The second exercise is to practice bringing your sense of sight to the present. This exercise is an exercise in deep eye-gazing without verbal communication. Find a partner interested in exploring this sense with you and sit facing one another. Look deeply into each other's eyes; can you drown in the sea of the other person's eyes? Can you sense the other's Soul deep within the ocean of their eyes?

Touch

This exercise in the sense of touch is best practiced with a partner. While one partner has their eyes closed, the other will lead them to various different objects. As your guide leads you to various objects, with your eyes closed, feel the texture, dimensions, boundaries, and quality of various objects. If you were a blind person, how would you imagine a rock by just feeling it? Bring all your awareness into your sense of touch.

Smell

With eyes closed, smell a flower or a fruit. Focus your sense of smell so you can pick up various scents or subtleties within the main scent of the flower or fruit. How many different fragrances can you pick up within the main smell of a flower or a fruit?

Taste

With your eyes closed, chew very slowly on a piece of fruit. Sense the chewing motion of your jaw. Feel the juice running down your throat; feel various tastes on your tongue (sour, sweet, bitter, etc.); sense the flow of saliva in your mouth.

Exercise—Resistance to the Present Moment

This exercise requires a partner. Each partner will have 5 minutes to complain about present life circumstances and shortcomings. Each partner will describe everything that they need in order to be truly happy in the future. After you have complained about what you do not have, take a moment to close your eyes and sense the state of your inner body. Most people feel an energy loss and a sense of frustration after complaining and resisting the present moment.

Meditation in Nature

Wander into nature and stay present. Staying present means just observing "what is" without labeling the flower or animal you are looking at. As you notice everything, make an effort not to label or categorize anything. Labeling and categorizing arise from the analytical mind. If necessary, close your eyes to bring deeper awareness to this moment in nature. Listen to the sound of the wind moving through the leaves, the sound of a running stream, or the song of a bird; pay attention to your own breathing, then, your body weight shifting from your heels to your toes as you stroll. One pleasant exercise that many of us have naturally done when we were children is to lie on our back and gaze at passing clouds— lost in their floating movement.

Summary of Exercises—Coming Back to the Present Moment

Here is a summary of various techniques you can use to step back into the present moment:

- Check in and observe your thoughts, your breath, emotions, and inner physical body. What is going on in your body? How are you breathing? What are you feeling? Observe your passing thoughts without being identified with them.

- During the day, occasionally ask yourself, "Am I present?" Just asking this question will bring you back to the NOW.

- If you cannot go to sleep, spend a few minutes listening to the sound of silence. You can plug your ears by placing your index fingers into your ears. Then, listen to that sound of silence within. Listen deeply to the sound of silence and your mind will dive into a vast space of emptiness.

- Imagine yourself as a hungry cat vigilantly watching a mouse hole. Ask yourself, I wonder what thought will come out of the mouse hole—(the portal of my mind)? Whenever a thought arises, let your exhalation blow that thought out of your nostrils then, await the next thought with the same vigilance and anticipation.

- Surrender to "what is" in this present moment. Do not resist what is going on NOW. Work with the moment not against it. This habit will reduce your resistance to life.

- Take a walk and during your walk, observe the smallest details—trees, leaves, sound of birds, the weight of your body on your feet, your breath, different smells, and any sensations pulsating in you. When in nature, do not label or categorize anything. Labeling and categorizing are mental habits that take away the charm of the moment. Instead of labeling, simply remain in silent presence of nature and observe without labeling, categorizing, or analyzing.

- Focus all your five senses on the present moment. Hear all sounds, as many sights as your eyes can absorb, feel the touch of your clothes against your skin. Do not label, categorize, or interpret anything with your mind. Don't think, just feel! Over and over again, leave your thinking mind and step into your feeling body.

Lesson 2

Healthy Breathing Awareness and Control of the Breath

Healthy breathing renders immense benefit to our physical, mental, emotional, and spiritual wellbeing. There is a very close connection between the mind and the body. There is also a very close relationship between your breathing and your mind. Through breath control we achieve mind control and self-control. Through awareness and control of the breath, we transform our mental restlessness into concentration and clarity.

Those who meditate on the breath regularly develop natural stamina, grace, and overall wellbeing. Regulation of the breath sets the pace for our mind, heart, and autonomous nervous system. When we consciously breathe slow, rhythmic, long, and deep breaths, our mind and nervous system naturally calm down.

Breath is the Source of Life and Consciousness

Breath brings in energy, or the Life Force that maintains all our body functions as well as our mental activity. Essentially, what comes in with each breath is life itself. Breath is the source of consciousness, and consciousness is the same Life Force that sustains the body, the mind, and the entire universe. Therefore, through breath, humans bring into the body the subatomic Life Force also known as *Prana, Chi, Qi or*

Holy Spirit. From the Yogic perspective P*rana* animates our body and mind; it gives life to all our organs, thoughts, words, and actions.

Breath is the Doorway Between the Visible and Invisible Worlds

Breath is the doorway between the visible and invisible worlds. That means that you can feel something coming in through your nostrils or your mouth with each breath, but you cannot see what is entering your body.

When a human dies, it is P*rana* that leaves the body, not oxygen. A dead set of lungs are still full of oxygen but devoid of *Prana* (Life).

Breath Awareness Supports Living in the Present Moment

As we explored in Lesson 1 (Living in the Present Moment), one of our biggest challenges on the spiritual journey is to live in the present moment. Awareness of the breath strengthens our concentration and makes the mind one-pointed. Breath awareness always brings us back to the present moment which is the only timeframe that we can truly work with.

Each time we become aware of our breathing, our mind chatter and worries dissolve — we are transported back to the present moment where we can make more accurate decisions appropriate to the needs of the present moment, not based on past mental conditioning. Whenever you are lost in thought, bring your focus back to your breath coming in and breath going out — your mind chatter will stop and you will experience concentration and clarity.

Breath Awareness and Meditation are Complementary

Just as breath awareness benefits meditation, meditation enhances healthy breathing. Breath awareness is an essential prerequisite to meditation. Meditation on the breath is one of the most powerful and natural meditation techniques. Since we can transport our breathing everywhere, breathing meditation is mobile. Meditation Guides instruct students to always be aware of their incoming and outgoing breaths.

People who do not meditate breathe predominantly through one nostril at any given time. Every 90 minutes, their body automatically alternates the dominant nostril. After some breath meditation practice you will notice that you breathe evenly through both nostrils; this happens to advanced meditators who are in control of their mind. When you breathe evenly through both nostrils, your mind becomes very clear and concentrated. This is because each nostril feeds P*rana* to the hemisphere of the brain that lies opposite that nostril. For instance, when you are breathing most of the air through your left nostril, you are nourishing the right lobe of your brain which is responsible for intuition, creativity, innovation, the Sixth Sense, etc. When you breathe into the right nostril, you are vitalizing the left side of the brain which is the lobe responsible for rational and analytical thinking. Finally, when you begin to breathe evenly through both nostrils, both hemispheres of your brain evenly receive the Life Force (P*rana*).

The Benefit of Long, Deep, Slow, Rhythmic Breaths

Long, deep, slow, rhythmic breaths into the stomach epitomize healthy breathing. As noted above, healthy breathing positively impacts us spiritually. Healthy breathing also promotes mental, physical, and emotional wellbeing.

Meditating on the breath softens and regulates the breath. As a result of breath awareness, our respiration rate becomes slower and with a slower respiration rate, our mind chatter ceases. In the ancient Indian spiritual texts it is written that the slower you breathe, the clearer and calmer your mind will be. Also, the slower your respiration rate, the longer you live. Essentially, *Breathlessness is deathlessness*; this is the well kept secret of calm, centered, and ageless people. Remember, the slower you breathe, the quieter your mind will be. Therefore, purposely slow down your respiration rate when you are tense or drowning in worrisome thoughts.

There are several physiological benefits to exercising healthy breathing. Rapid and shallow breathing in the chest, the alternative to breathing into the stomach, damages the heart, agitates the mind, and throws the nervous system off balance. Avoid breathing into the chest; chest breathing increases the acid-to-base ratio in our blood and when acidic blood circulates in the brain, the mind becomes very agitated. Also, the lungs of chest breathers become top heavy, especially in old age when we stubbornly settle into old habits having forgotten that as children we used to naturally breathe into our stomachs.

Healthy breathing also benefits us emotionally. Our breathing patterns are a direct reflection of our emotional states. Observe someone's breathing and you will know their inner emotional state. For instance, we gasp when we are amazed, choke when we are extremely sad, and sigh when we are relieved. We breathe rapid, short breaths when we are angry. Our breath is shallow, jerky, and fast during periods of anger, fear, and excess excitement. During periods of deep concentration we experience Theta brain waves which equate to 3.5 cycles per second on an EEG machine. In this state our breath naturally becomes rhythmic, deep, slow, and steady. During deep meditation, the breath becomes so tiny and still that it seems you are hardly breathing at all. If you experience this kind of feeble respiration, do not worry, it will not lead to suffocation. Your slow respiration rate is simply a reflection of your state of deep relaxation and the drop in your metabolic rate.

The Qualities of Healthy Breathing

Healthy breathing exhibits these six qualities:

- Long
- Deep
- Smooth
- Rhythmic
- Slow
- Quiet

Unhealthy breathing has the following qualities:

- Jerky
- Rapid
- Shallow
- Noisy
- Long pause between inhalation and exhalation

Each count for your inhalation and exhalation is approximately one second. Regulate your breathing so that your exhalations are nearly twice as long as your inhalations. The long pause between inhalation and exhalation is especially distracting to the mind. Try to establish a steady and even rhythm between inhalation and exhalation. Only in very advanced *pranayama* techniques do practitioners exercise long pauses between breaths.

Remember, the best place to breathe into is your stomach. Relocate your breathing from your chest down to your stomach. Diaphragmatic breathing into the stomach increases the base ratio of the blood flowing to the brain which calms the mind and nervous system.

Breathing Exercises

When doing breathing exercises, wear loose fitting, comfortable clothes. Do away with belts and tight collars. The optimal kind of breathing is the diaphragmatic breath. During diaphragmatic breathing, your stomach, sides of your ribcage, as well as your torso move outward as your inhale. As you exhale, your stomach retracts toward your spine, your shoulders drop, and your ribcage retracts back to its normal size.

During breathing meditation, do not tilt your head; your head, neck, and spine should be in vertical alignment. Relax your tongue and rest the tip of your tongue against the back of your top teeth. Practice pushing out your lower abdomen during inhalations and pulling it in during exhalations. During inhalations, experience a yawn-like sensation. During exhalations, envision your breath draining through a hole located at the pit of your stomach.

You should feel confident that breathing into the stomach does not create a fat and flabby stomach. If anything, these exercises will strengthen your abdominal muscles so that you can pull in your stomach at any time you wish.

Diaphragmatic Breathing into the Stomach

Lie down on your back and place your hand on your stomach. Take 15 deep, slow, rhythmic breaths into your stomach. Make sure your stomach and the hand resting on your stomach rise and fall during each breath. During diaphragmatic breathing, the sides of your body are also expanding and contracting with each breath. It is very important that your exhalations are twice as long as your inhalations; whenever your exhalations are twice as long as your inhalations, your mind and nervous system become steady and centered.

Again, each count of the breath typically lasts approximately one second.

The Crocodile Pose

Lie on your stomach and rest your forehead on your forearms. As you inhale, sense your stomach pushing off and against the floor. As you lay on your stomach breathing this way, your lower back should be moving and curling slightly upward with each inhalation.

Ujjayi Breathing

Ujjayi breathing fills the body with vitality, calms the nerves, deepens your respiration, and reduces the acidity of your blood, rendering your blood more alkaline. During *Ujjayi* breathing practice long, deep, and even respiration. Long *Ujjayi* breaths purify and rejuvenate the brain, nervous system, and all internal organs. You will also increase your lung capacity by breathing into your stomach.

As mentioned in Lesson 1 (Living in the Present Moment), to practice the *Ujjayi* breath, you need to squeeze a muscle at the back of your throat called the glottis. This is like squeezing the two sides of the throat together and breathing. The sound of *Ujjayi* is as if you are whispering a silent "AH" or a hissing sound from the back of your throat. While exercising *Ujjayi* breathing, hear the sound of "AH" in your throat without opening your mouth. Sometimes it helps if you touch the tip of your tongue against your palate.

The Lock Exercise

After 5 minutes of regular *Ujjayi* breathing, do five rounds of *Ujjayi* breathing while following this instruction: Take a deep

Ujjayi breath into your stomach; as you inhale your chin should descend and touch your chest. When the chin reaches the chest, tighten your anal muscles, pull your genitals upward, and hold your breath in. This motion feels like your stomach goes in toward your spinal column.

When you need to inhale again first raise your chin back up while exhaling the previous breath. Now, take another deep *Ujjayi* breath into your stomach. Then, the chin descends on the chest, you tighten the anal muscles, pull your stomach toward your spinal column, and hold the breath in until the next round. Repeat this cycle five times.

Fire Breathing

Fire breathing will inject your body with a massive dosage of Life Force.

In this exercise, you inhale deeply, then imagine you are blowing a dust particle out of both your nostrils with a short and sudden jet of air as you exhale. As you jet the air out of your nostrils, your stomach should snap inward.

Do three rounds of fire breathing with five fire-breaths per round.

Witnessing the Breath

In this exercise, you will take away your willpower.

Lie on your back, and just witness the body's instinct to breathe when it wants to. Do not analyze or interfere with the instinctual rhythm of breathing. Just witness when the body wants to breathe; almost like you are surprised each time the breath comes. Just observe—you are not in charge.

Take a very slow, long exhalation and keep breathing out until every bit of breath is out. Now, put your conscious willpower aside, just lie back and let your body surprise you with its next inhalation. Do the same during the exhalation; yield to the body's instinct to exhale—let each exhalation surprise you. Relax all muscles and visualize all thoughts rushing out of your nostrils with each exhalation.

If any thoughts come to you, gently put your awareness back on witnessing the next inhalation and exhalation. Completely yield to the body's instinct to breathe.

Breathing with Chin Down

Breathing with your chin down on your chest puts pressure on the carotid arteries that carry blood to the brain. This form of breathing brings about a deep sense of quietude right before extended periods of meditation.

Sit in a yogic position with your head, neck and spine in vertical alignment. Touch your first finger with your thumb in order to close the body's circuit and allow Prana to circulate. Do 10 of these breaths, pointing your chin down. Don't forget to breathe into your abdomen with slow, long, deep, smooth, and rhythmic breaths.

Breathe in with 4 counts and exhale with 6 counts.

Alternate Nostril Breathing (5-minute-exercise)

This exercise is very effective for balancing the left and right hemispheres of your brain. You probably know that the right side of the brain is associated with creativity, intuition, innovation, and art. The left hemisphere is associated with linear logic, math, science, and your analytical capabilities.

As mentioned earlier, every 90 minutes the body automatically alternates the dominant nostril through which you are breathing. Each nostril nourishes that lobe of your brain that lies opposite to that nostril (right nostril feeds the left brain hemisphere and vice versa). If you are calm and focused, it means that your left nostril is currently dominant and nourishing the right hemisphere of your brain. Right nostril dominance creates aggressiveness and intense physical activity.

In this exercise, you will balance out the two hemispheres of your brain by breathing into the nostril located on the opposite side of the brain lobe which you are energizing.

To reach very profound levels of meditation, the student needs to achieve an equal flow of breath through both nostrils. Do not concern yourself with this notion. As your meditation becomes deeper, the flow of air through both nostrils will automatically even out and flow with equal force.

Get comfortable in a chair or in an erect sitting posture on the floor. Your head, neck, and spine should be in vertical alignment.

Close your eyes and relax while doing five full round-belly breaths. Do not do Ujjayi breaths in this exercise. Relax your stomach muscles and breathe into your stomach.

Now raise your left hand up to face level and close off the right nostril with the index finger of your left hand (keeping the left nostril open), then inhale and exhale once through the open (left) nostril. (See illustration below.)

Now close off the left nostril (the one you just breathed through), with the thumb of your left hand, and inhale and exhale once through the right open nostril.

Alternate nostrils after each round of inhalation and exhalation. Do this practice for 5 full minutes.

Lesson 3

Meditation: Practice and Benefits

Just as our nervous system has the capability to make us tense when we perceive a threat or danger, we also have the natural capacity to slip into quietude and ease through a *Relaxation Response*.

Patanjali, one of the founding fathers of the science of Yoga, taught that meditation is stillness of the mind. Meditation is the practice of using the mind to dive deep within itself in order to transcend fleeting thoughts. The human mind and nervous system is the only one amongst all species that can transcend and witness itself from a higher altitude. No animal can witness its own mind.

Any human activity that causes time and space to disappear is a form of meditation. For example, a grandfather in love with his grandchild may lose track of time while playing with the beloved child. This is a form of meditation because the grandfather is in love and loses track of time. The feeling of deep love changes human brain waves, our respiratory rate, and our metabolic rate; deep meditation exhibits the same physiological changes.

Different Depths of Meditation

To arouse a state of deep concentration, we need to focus the mind for 12 seconds on a single subject of meditation. This 12-second period of non-thought or a singular focused thought, is considered concentration. As we go from the normal waking state to a state of concentration, our brain waves slow down from busy Beta waves (15-16 hertz) to calmer Alpha waves (8-13 hertz). If we can multiply our 12-second period of concentration by 12 (144 seconds or 2.4 minutes), we experience deep meditation. Any practitioner can do this by focusing the mind on a single object of meditation. For example, movement of the breath is one of the most natural subjects to meditate on.

During deep meditation, our brain waves become even calmer and we experience Theta waves (3.5-8 hertz). Theta waves represent the state of consciousness right before we fall asleep. The difference between sleep and deep meditation is that during deep meditation you are just as relaxed as deep sleep, yet, you are fully awake and present.

The depth of meditation can continue to where a meditator is completely absorbed in a non-thought state of clarity and quietude for 28.8 minutes. In such a state, our brain waves subside to Delta waves that are extremely calm (0.5 cycles per second). In Sanskrit spiritual terms, 28.8 minutes of non-thought is called *Samadhi*. In this state, the sense of the individual "I" dissolves into one universal throb pulsating within all of space.

Two Primary Categories of Meditation

Within all the spiritual traditions, there are essentially two categories of meditation. Although each category has distinct characteristics, both paths meet at the end. The two primary categories of meditation are:

1. **Mindfulness:** In this kind of meditation we train our concentration muscles so that we become mindful of life events; we become aware of mental, emotional, and physical impulses as they arise and pass away with each moment. There is no

other underlying motive other than awakening to *what is*, in the passing moment.

2. **Concentration:** Whereas in mindfulness meditation we continuously focus on whatever is happening in the present moment, in the path of concentration meditation, we concentrate the mind again and again on a specific object of meditation, such as a *mantra* or our breath until we become fully absorbed by that meditation. Within this path, the concentrated mind turns inward on itself and continues a downward dive to such depth that ultimately, we no longer identify with the body, mind, and five senses. In such deep states of relaxation, *Kundalini Shakti*, the subatomic Life Force lying dormant at the base of the spinal column, begins to rise up the spine. The masters of this path state that true spiritual progress begins with the awakening of the dormant *Kundalini Shakti*.

By practicing either of the two categories of meditation, mindfulness or concentration, we focus our mind and disentangle ourselves from passing thoughts and emotions. A focused mind is naturally clear and joyful; disentangled from passing thoughts and emotions, we become clear, focused, free, and more loving.

As we continue to practice meditation, we travel further toward a silent inner space where we become aware of our subtle intentions, thoughts, emotions, and physical sensations. The more you meditate, the subtler your awareness becomes; you will develop a powerful inner radar that can tune into the subtlest internal as well as external forces.

Karma, the Boomerang Effect

Practice slipping into the gap between two thoughts, or focus on the rest between two breaths. Slipping into this gap enables us to release the thoughts of our mind and resist entangling our self in the constant undulation of passing thoughts and emotions.

After all, it is movement of the mind that causes us to react; first the mind moves, then we experience emotions, and finally, the body springs into action in response to our emotions. Nature then returns a reaction similar to our actions in a boomerang fashion. This boomerang effect is what Yogis call *Karma*; for every action there is an equivalent reaction. By establishing yourself in the calm between two breaths, you can prevent a negative cycle of action-reaction.

Kundalini Shakti

Kundalini Shakti is the Sanskrit name which refers to the subatomic God Force lying dormant about six centimeters above the base of our spinal column. We are able to awaken *Kundalini Shakti* through the grace of a Master. Once enlivened, *Kundalini Shakti* flows freely through our body, piercing our seven main energy centers (*chakras*) and then spreading outward through the 72,000 tiny channels (*nadis*) through which this spiritual electricity (Life Force) circulates within our body. In cleansing these 72,000 channels, *Kundalini re*vitalizes your body, heals negative and stuck emotions, and accesses parts of your brain previously inaccessible.

Kundalini energy is dormant in most people until awakened by a spiritual master and spiritual practices such as Kriya Yoga meditation and *Pranayama* (breath-control). During meditation, *Kundalini* rises through the spinal column from the root *chakra*, at the base of the spine, to the fontanel located at the top-center of the head.

Emotional Benefits of Meditation

Meditation decreases worry, anxiety, and over indulgence in addictive elements by eliminating inner restlessness.

Through meditation we are able to hear our inner voice, i.e. our personal truth. When we are clear about who we are, we can choose our life priorities and not waste time with an endless number of daily or life distractions. Instead of living in confusion and going around in circles, we begin to truly grow and progress in life. This is because, ultimately, meditation increases our self-love.

Physiological Benefits of Meditation

During meditation, our respiratory rate slows down. In fact, all aspects of body metabolism slow down, requiring less oxygen. This deceleration of breathing and metabolic functions, in turn, quiets the mind and conserves energy. The slowdown in body metabolism also prolongs your lifespan because your internal organs experience less *w*ear and tear.

During deep meditation, we are in a state of restful alertness. The following are symptoms of restful alertness:
- Body and senses relaxed, yet fully awake and aware
- Loss of any sense of self-consciousness; absence of any sense of social personality
- The brain vibrates at Alpha or Theta states rather than the busy Beta state

- A sense of losing track of time and space
- Body metabolism drops to a minimum
- A drop in heartbeat rate
- Blood pressure normalizes
- Slow, deep, and rhythmic breathing
- Deactivation of the parietal lobes of the brain that register outside sensory information. Instead of being distracted by outside sensory input, we tune into our inner world and inner wisdom (inward gaze).
- Neurons in the brain adapt themselves to the frontal, concentration area of the brain thus increasing our power of concentration manifold

Most importantly, the vibrational frequency of our body increases; consciousness leaves the dense physical layer of flesh and bones (vibrating at 350 cycles per second) and moves outward to the more subtle and invisible energy layers, finally extending toward our sixth energy layer (the Soul), vibrating above one million cycles per second. Higher vibrational energy means more vitality, joy, and higher consciousness. At such high vibrational frequencies, we are able to harmonize ourselves with creative forces which create any positive opportunity that we focus on in the material world. All divine experiences occur at the higher vibrational frequencies of the body.

Spiritual Benefits of Meditation

During deep meditation the vibrational frequency of our body rises. This means that our spiritual energy increases during meditation. During deep meditation, we transform from the solid body into the lighter energy layers surrounding the solid body. This is like a block of ice melting into water and finally evaporating into gaseous fog. So, essentially, meditation is the process of de-atomizing through a rapid increase in our vibrational frequency. The higher your energetic vibrations, the closer you are to God Consciousness which is an energy vibrating above one million cycles per second.

Through meditation, you can move beyond the limitations of your mind. The mind cannot absorb anything beyond its own past experiences. When you transcend the mind, and slip into the silent gap between two thoughts, you will have access to new dimensions of thought, higher knowledge and higher powers such as: clairvoyance, intuition, telekinesis (moving objects with your mind), etc.

The more quiet your mind becomes, the less attached you will be to external distractions. As you become more inward and less distracted by externalities, your nervous system becomes steadier and you attain unwavering centeredness. In fact, scientific studies prove that meditators have very focused, yet flexible minds.

Meditation Changes Our Outlook and Responses

As we practice meditating we develop the power to change the way we perceive and respond to life situations. The reason we can do this is because meditation develops our ability to witness and not react to unconscious and unwanted habits. As we become free of habitual and conditioned negative responses, many more choices open up in our lives. This is one of the most beneficial gifts of meditation.

Through meditation we learn to surrender and trust the natural flow of the universe. Instead of changing our environment or circumstances, we are able to watch and change our mind's reaction to each situation. We realize that as we change our state of mind, we experience the situation differently. Remember this formula; write it down and review it every day:

Circumstances + My Reaction = Result

Your life will change once you learn to change your mental reaction to events. Contrary to what your ego might believe, you are not in control of all of life's events. The only thing you can control is your mental perception and mental reaction to each event. In spiritual terms, the definition of a fool is the person who continues to react the same way over and over again, while expecting life results to change.

Specific Guidelines and Considerations for Meditation

Faith and love

Meditation requires sincerity, discipline, desire for God, and love of the Self (Soul). Without these, meditation becomes a burdensome chore. I would say nothing deepens meditation as much as deep faith in the existence of the God Force within your body and within every element of the universe. Simply focusing on techniques will render your spiritual practice dry and emotionless; faith and love are key to deepening your spiritual practice. Love your inner God and your meditation will be deep. Conversely, meditate deeply and you will fall in love with God.

Awareness of Breath

As discussed in Lesson 2 (Healthy Breathing), awareness and regulation of your breath is an essential prerequisite to deep meditation.

Prior to meditation, practice 5 minutes of deep, long, smooth, rhythmic and slow *Ujjayi* breathing. *Ujjayi* breathing quickly calms the mind and prepares it for deep meditation; it also activates waves of *Kundalini* energy along the spine. While taking *Ujjayi* breaths, make sure you breathe into your stomach, not your chest.

The *Ujjayi* breath is a special breathing technique practiced in *Kriya* Yoga which helps us connect with *Prana* circulating in our body. Refer to Lesson 2 (Healthy Breathing) for details on healthy breathing, including the *Ujjayi* breath.

Correct Meditative Posture

Our meditative posture is crucial to proper circulation of P*rana* through the spine and the rest of the body.

To practice a correct meditative posture, ensure your head, neck, and spine are in vertical alignment. This posture allows for the P*rana* (Life Force) to flow up the spinal column with greater ease. Your sitting posture should be stable as well as comfortable. In other words, find a comfortable position that is not painful; all pain and discomfort distracts you from deep meditation.

Once you are sitting comfortably with your head, neck and spine in vertical alignment, touch the tip of your thumb with the tip of the first finger and close your eyes. The last two actions close the body's circuitry so that the Life Force can circulate within your body without spilling out into space.

Stillness of the body is also critical. When the body moves, the mind moves. Inversely, when the mind thinks, the body moves.

Helpful Attitudes toward Meditation

During meditation, relax completely—do not try to relax, just let go and melt into your breath. Surrender to any sensations; witness thoughts, emotions, and physical sensations without judging or reacting to them. Never be angry at the mind for creating thoughts. The mind is like a little child, or a kitten—all it knows is how to be playful. The nature of any mind is to jump from one thought to another. As you meditate, you should be like a loving parent watching over the playful mind. Just continue to bring back the playful mind to the object of meditation.

During meditation, sit with a loving, patient smile, and simply observe whatever occurs. Do not be entangled, identified, or frustrated by the mental chatter. Never try to block out any specific thought or emotion. Whatever thought or emotion you resist or try to block out will stick to you like glue!

Understand that the light of God and supreme calmness is always within you; it is thinly veiled by your mind chatter. As soon as your thoughts perish, you experience the vast, silent emptiness of Pure Consciousness (your Soul). So, do not try to "get there"; you are already there; it is simply a matter of your false identification with the mind chatter instead of identifying with the deep silence that lies between two thoughts or two breaths.

The way to stilling the mind is to simply observe the mind. Observing the mind means having the Witness (Pure Consciousness) diligently watch the screen of the mind. As soon as Pure Consciousness casts its light on the mind, the chattering mind disappears and becomes one with the silence of Pure Consciousness. One very effective practice for witnessing the mind is to stare at the screen of the mind as if you are watching a movie; second-by-second wait for the next thought to arise. If this is done correctly, you will see that the next thought never arrives as long as you are intensely awaiting that next thought.

Whatever you focus on during meditation becomes amplified. Do not focus on your wounds or darkness. Instead, focus deeply on your inner light and you will experience just that. Remember, the light of God is already shining within every atom of your body; you do not have to achieve any goals to "get there." Just be conscious that you are already *there*.

Other Considerations for Deepening Meditation

Physical activity helps the process of meditation. Some exercise, being in nature, and healthy daily activity that consumes your physical energy enhances the depth of your meditation. It is good to be a little physically tired prior to meditation practice.

Never go into meditation with any expectations. If you are tracking your own inner state, or conscious of extraordinary experiences you will not experience deep meditation. Meditation is total release and letting go to whatever may occur. Let the meditation take you where it will. Be as innocent as a child.

When you notice that thoughts are there, gently put your focus back on the object of meditation such as your *mantra*, breath, inner light, etc. At a silent point during meditation, you may feel the vibration or sensation of the *mantra* within your body. Become aware of the location where your *mantra* is vibrating. This is an area you need to pay attention to.

In the beginning, you will experience various emotions like anger, jealousy, over sensitivity, and fear. Sometimes you will sense involuntary movements (*kriyas*). All these are just impurities within your nervous system that meditation is bringing up to the surface. Let the fire of meditation burn all the impurities of the ego, mind, and body.

Depth of meditation also depends on your emotional state. Emotional blockages interfere with smooth meditation. The more emotionally open, the less defensive, the deeper your meditation will be. Understand that the true Yogi must walk through his personal hell, made up of past hurts and negativities. Do not be fooled by those who preach that you can go from extreme inner pain straight into bliss by just meditating. The word *tapas* means heat; anyone serious about personal growth must have the courage to "cook" in the heat of daily spiritual practice.

Even if you are experiencing powerful emotions, just open up and let them flow through you. As long as you accept everything and do not block emotional or mental energy, your meditation will go smoothly.

The mind is conditioned to jump from thought to thought. If your mind resists meditation, say to your mind *this is not time for thinking, we need to be with our inner God now. When we are done, you can go back to thinking.*

What to Meditate On

The object of meditation can be a sound, light, body sensations, the breath, a *mantra*—anything that your mind is attracted to and rejoices in. The more attracted you are to the object of meditation, the deeper will be your concentration. So, choose to meditate on an object or subject that truly fascinates and delights you.

Some *mantras* carry a special vibrational sound that fascinates the mind; the mind listens more closely to the *mantra* until the mind loses itself in the vibrations of the *mantra*. At this point, you are in total silence. This silence is called *Pure Consciousness*. Pure Consciousness is the source of all memory, creativity, and thought.

The best object of meditation is the Self—the inner God. Worship your own Soul and you will never be tired of meditating.

When and Where to Meditate

It is best to practice meditation for twenty minutes twice a day. The best hours to practice in the morning are between 5-6 AM. The next meditation should ideally be done before dinner in the early evening.

The stomach should be empty during meditative practice. Meditate at least three hours after a meal. Of course, the busy professional can be more flexible and meditate two hours after the end of a meal.

Such measures are ideal because after a meal time much of your blood, enzymes, and muscular activity are around your digestive system thereby reducing the amount of your energy and focus on the spinal column and your mind. This is why you will want to wait after a meal before meditating.

The devoted meditators typically dedicate a clean corner of their homes to meditation and prayer. In such sanctuaries you do not smoke or drink alcohol.

It is best to face East during meditation. The reason for this is that during specific hours the electromagnetic force of the Earth emanating from the eastward direction is very powerful and conducive to deep meditation.

Surrendering to Meditation

Surrendering to your meditation is essential to experiencing deeper states of meditation. Meditation begins when the meditator dies, or when the meditator fully surrenders all sense of "I", ego and mind.

Some beginning meditators find it challenging to surrender to their meditation. Rather than jumping right into meditation with a sense of needing to accomplish something, try to take a few minutes to relax into your meditation. It can be beneficial to start with 5 minutes of deep *Ujjayi* breathing in the stomach to help relax your mind and body. You might also take a few minutes to relax all your muscles, releasing tension with each exhalation. Imagine each wave of exhalation washing away all your thoughts. Finally, try putting your awareness on the object of your meditation such as your breath, a *mantra*, or light, and then sink into meditation.

Continue to ride each exhalation into nothingness. Each and every time you meditate, totally let go and be lost in your meditation. Surrender and allow your meditation to take you wherever it may.

Obstacles to Meditation

Scattered Mind

The scattered mind jumps from one thought to another. Worry and doubt are results of the scattered mind. Continued and regular practice of meditation focuses the scattered mind.

Foggy or Dull Mind

A foggy and dull mind cannot concentrate on the object of meditation. When your mind is foggy and dull you experience a sense of boredom during meditation. If this is your present condition, you need to be diligently aware of passing thoughts and emotions during meditation. If you feel sleepy, take twenty rapid breaths into your stomach area and exhale a sharp jet of air out of your nostrils. Also, taking a cool shower prior to meditative practice is very helpful. When the skin pores are open and clean, your meditation will naturally be deeper.

No Commitment and/or Sincerity

Meditation takes willing commitment, and to be honest, is a daily and lifelong endeavor. The act of worship itself is very sincere. Meditation is really worship of one's Soul (inner God). Meditation must come from love of the heart; if you simply practice a technique without faith or sincerity, your meditation will become dry and intolerable.

No Concentration or Focus

No one can practice any spiritual techniques without a focused, concentrated mind. In fact, without concentration, we cannot achieve any success in life. This is why, in the beginning stages, the meditation master works on strengthening the student's concentration muscles.

No Faith or Courage

You need courage and strong belief that persistent, sincere meditation fosters inner quietude and higher consciousness, and that once you access higher consciousness, all material success will follow. Doubt renders two minds and a wise proverb says *you can never reach your destination riding two horses.*

Greed and Expectation

Do not look for any experience during meditation; go into each meditation with child-like innocence. Those who progress quickly are not seeking powers and ecstatic experiences; they meditate for the love of God and the love of their own higher Self.

Intellectual Analysis

The lower mind or intellect can never grasp higher consciousness experienced during transcendence. The brain needs to rest at the Alpha wave state rather than the busy Beta wave state before we can truly dive deep into meditation. Intellectual analysis keeps the brain active at the Beta wave frequency prohibiting the silent meditative state.

Pride and/or Regret

Trying to be the best meditator in the group, or regretting the loss of one or two powerful states of bliss is nothing but attachment and spiritual pride arising from egoism. The more you chase and long for divine experiences, the more God will elude you. The God-Force is fluid energy; She never repeats Herself, nor can you nail Her down during every meditation. Let go of everything that comes to you and you will have more and more divine experiences. Do not chase experiences; just love your inner Self.

Useful Hints for Deepening Meditation

Useful attitudes during meditation are:

- Practice sincerity, perseverance, dedication, and friendliness toward your mind and passing emotions.

- Do not let anything enter your mind without witnessing that visitor – be it a thought, emotion, or mental image.

- Stay very attentive and awake during meditation. Meditation is the art of inner listening; you do not have to strain, just tune into whatever is happening in the present moment. When you notice that you have thoughts, over and over again, bring your focus back to the object of meditation such as your breath or *mantra*.

- Be patient. Clear observation of the mind is a lifetime endeavor. Mindfulness disentangles you from impermanent thoughts, emotions, and physical sensations.

- Remember all states of meditation are impermanent. Thoughts, emotions, and physical sensations are impermanent waves of energy that arise and disappear.

- Do not resist negative or shallow meditations (aversion) and do not become attached to deep meditation (attachment). Both aversion and attachment cause pain and bring you out of deep meditation.

- Understand there is no fixed identity of Self. You are a fluid energy field that changes from moment to moment. With each exhalation, release your identification with fixed roles such as *mother, architect, Indian, man, woman, housewife.*

- Realize that the only part of us that is constant is the Witness. Pure Consciousness is that Witness. Pure Consciousness is ever awake and alert, even during deep meditation.

- Know yourself. During meditation, let your consciousness be awake and aware. Pay attention to all physical sensations, passing emotions and thoughts. Also pay attention to changes in your breathing including the various qualities as well as the start, length, pause, and end of your breath.

- Let whatever arises flow through you. Stay completely open to whatever occurs during meditation. Do not try to block or resist anything. Remember, you actually energize and strengthen whatever you are trying to resist.

- Surrender to the breath and let the mind sway on the motion of the breath. Give up trying to relax; trying is the ego's way of resisting meditation.

- Whatever arises during meditation, release it with the next exhalation. As you release both pleasant and unpleasant sensations, you will feel very expanded and joyous.

- If you experience fear or pain during meditation, look that fear straight in the eyes. If you face your fearful emotions directly, you will see that fear disappears; this is because fear is just an illusion of the mind. Fears are not real—face them, experience them and they will disintegrate!

- During meditation, do not analyze your problems. Whatever you analyze and focus on will become bigger and stronger. Just let go of your thinking mind with each exhalation.

Lesson 4

Kriya Yoga

Kriya Yoga is a very powerful and advanced form of yoga. It is known as one of the more direct routes toward enlightenment or establishing a sacred union between individual and Cosmic Consciousness. In ancient India, only advanced students who had previously practiced other forms of yoga were initiated into Kriya Yoga.

The Father of Kriya Yoga

The advanced and ancient yogic practice of Kriya Yoga was introduced for the betterment of civilization by one of the most revered yogis of all time—Kriya Babaji Nagaraj.

Although Kriya Babaji Nagaraj, lovingly referred to as Babaji by his disciples, has not been in his physical body for some 500 years, many sages such as Paramahansa Yogananda (*Autobiography of a Yogi*), have had visions of Babaji. Those who have had direct visions of Babaji claim that the Spirit of Babaji resides in the Himalayan caves near the village of Badrinath, along with the spirits of his sister and a dozen disciples. It is said that this 'holy band of sages' continue to wander about as invisible, formless bodies of light, bestowing grace upon a chaotic world.

The Power of Kriya Yoga

This powerful form of meditation magnetizes every cell and molecule of your body. Kriya Yoga gently awakens the atomic energy of *Kundalini Shakti* which was discussed in detail in Lesson 3 (Meditation and Its Benefits).

The ancient techniques of Kriya Yoga awaken *Kundalini* in a very gentle manner, one *chakra* at a time. There is no danger of experiencing adverse effects of *Kundalini* rising and cleansing your energy centers and channels as long as your Kriya Yoga master is fully realized with his *Kundalini Shakti* awakened.

Once *Kundalini* awakens in your body through the grace of a realized master, all of your life will change – materially and spiritually. This is the power of Kriya Yoga.

The Technique of Kriya Yoga

Kriya Yoga involves plenty of visualization as the practitioner often envisions circulation of vitalizing breath in and around various energy centers (*chakras*). You cannot apply dry ration or logic in this practice since most of the techniques utilized in Kriya Yoga involve creative visualization and a concentrated inward focus.

Kriya Yoga engages the practitioner in circulation of energized breath in and around the 72,000 energy channels or *nadis* referred to in the previous lesson. In Kriya Yoga practice, we often use the *Ujjayi* breath described in Lesson 2 (Healthy Breathing) to energize the *nadis*.

The genius of Kriya Yoga lies in the fact that this ancient science disarms the rebellious and stubborn nature of the mind. You will notice during other forms of meditation practice, that if you strictly command your mind to *be quiet!!* your mind will resist and do just the opposite, creating restless havoc. Kriya Yoga does not ask the practitioner to be quiet at all. Rather, you are encouraged to let thoughts come and go freely like a rushing river as you sit quietly by the banks of this river of thought and watch the strong current with a smile. You simply witness thought. Whenever you notice you are identified with thoughts, you simply come back to visualization of your breath circulating in and around the *nadis*.

Basic Kriya Yoga Practice

In the science of Kriya Yoga, the order or sequence of the practice(s) is critical as are the number of rounds (times) that you perform each of the breathing practices. It is important to honor and respect this ancient knowledge. Please do not invent your own Kriya Yoga practices as this may disturb your physiological and psychological balance.

Pre-Meditation Relaxation and Emptying of Mind

Sit in the meditative posture described in Lesson 3 (Meditation – Practices and Benefits), with your head, neck, and spine in vertical alignment. Touch the tip of your first finger to the tip of your thumb.

Now, relax your stomach muscles. As you relax your stomach muscles, you will be able to transfer the movement of breath from your chest to your stomach. Belly-breathing will immediately relax your mind by changing the composition of your blood. Feel your stomach move up and down with each inhalation and exhalation.

As you sit and witness the movement of breath in your belly, purposely slow down your respiration (speed of your breathing), and make your exhalation twice as long as your inhalation.

Now, plug both ears with your fingertips, and begin the *Ujjayi* breaths. With eyes closed, and breathing very slow *Ujjayi* breaths, you have the option of inhaling as if the tide is coming upon the shore and exhaling as though the wave is merging back to its Source. Imagine that with each inhalation, you as an individual ego (person with a name) come up on the shore, and with each exhalation, the wave that is YOU merges back into empty space. Do this practice for 20 rounds.

Now, bring your focus to the point between your eyebrows. Purposely slow down your *Ujjayi* breaths. Create a very long gap between your inhalation and exhalation and pause. Within the gap between two breaths, and in your state of breathlessness, vigilantly await the arrival of the next thought. Stay very awake and breathless; as you await the next thought with curiosity and anticipation.

Chakra Vitalization

Though your seven *chakras* are amongst the 72,000 *nadis*, these seven *chakras* are major power stations. Energizing the seven *chakras* deepens your Kriya Yoga meditation greatly. Below are instructions on how to energize your *chakras*.

Bring your focus to the point between your eyebrows (Third Eye or *Ajna Chakra*). Now, take a deep *Ujjayi* breath into your Third Eye. Hold your *Ujjayi* breath as long as you can. Then, use two motions of exhalation to COMPLETELY empty your lungs. What I mean is exhale once to empty 80 percent of the air in your lungs, then, continue exhaling once more until there is not even a bit of breath left in you. In a state of complete breathlessness, remain focused on the point between your eyebrows and vigilantly await the arrival of the next thought. Repeat this exercise 10 times.

Bring your focus to the pit of your throat (*Vishuddha Chakra*). Now, take a deep *Ujjayi* breath into the pit of your throat. Hold your *Ujjayi* breath as long as you can. Then, use two motions of exhalation to COMPLETELY empty your lungs. In a state of complete breathlessness, remain focused on the lower part of your throat and vigilantly await the arrival of the next thought. Repeat this exercise 10 times.

Bring your focus to your heart (*Anahata Chakra*) in the middle of your chest cavity. Now, take a deep *Ujjayi* breath into your heart. Hold your *Ujjayi* breath as long as you can. Then, use two motions of exhalation to COMPLETELY empty your lungs. In a state of complete breathlessness, remain focused on your heart and vigilantly await the arrival of the next thought. Repeat this exercise 10 times.

Bring your focus to your navel (*Manipura Chakra*) in the middle of your abdomen, at the point of your umbilical cord. Then, take a deep *Ujjayi* breath into your navel. Hold your *Ujjayi* breath as long as you can. Then, use two motions of exhalation to COMPLETELY empty your lungs. In a state of complete breathlessness, remain focused on your navel, and vigilantly await the arrival of the next thought. Repeat this exercise 10 times.

Bring your focus to your lower stomach, the area between your navel and your sexual organs (*Svadhishthana Chakra*). Now, take a deep *Ujjayi* breath into this *chakra*. Hold your *Ujjayi* breath as long as you can. Then, use two motions of exhalation to COMPLETELY empty your lungs. In a state of complete breathlessness, remain focused on your lower stomach, and vigilantly await the arrival of the next thought. Repeat this exercise 10 times.

Bring your focus to your tailbone (*Muladhara Chakra*). Now, take a deep *Ujjayi* breath into this chakra. Hold your *Ujjayi* breath as long as you can. Now, use two motions of exhalation to

COMPLETELY empty your lungs. In complete breathlessness, remain focused on your tailbone, and vigilantly await the arrival of the next thought. Repeat this exercise 10 times.

Bring your focus to your crown, the top center of your head (*Sahasrara Chakra*). Now, take a deep *Ujjayi* breath into this *chakra*. Hold your *Ujjayi* breath as long as you can. Now, use two motions of exhalation to COMPLETELY empty your lungs. In a state of complete breathlessness, remain focused on the point at the top of your head, and vigilantly await the arrival of the next thought. Repeat this exercise 10 times.

Front-to-Back *Ujjayi* Breathing

In this exercise, we will circulate the *Ujjayi* breath up the front of the body, down the back of the body and back to the front again. Repeat the sequence of instructions below for 29 rounds.

Bring your attention to your lower stomach. Imagine the *Ujjayi* inhalation rising from your lower stomach to your navel, to your heart, to the pit of your throat, to the point between your eyebrows.

Pause for a very long time while concentrating on the point between your eyebrows.

Next, imagine the exhalation flowing to the back of your skull through the parting of your hair directly behind your head. In Kriya Yoga that parting behind your skull is named *Bindu* and is said to be the point at which your Soul first enters your physical body.

After you exhalation out *Bindu*, inhale the breath back into *Bindu*.

Finally, exhale down the back of your body as if the exhalation flows from the top of your spinal column down to your tailbone.

Spiraling *Ujjayi* Breath Up the Spine

Bring your focus to your tailbone. As you take a deep *Ujjayi* breath, imagine your inhalation spiraling up your spinal column like a whirlwind. Breathe very slowly in this exercise as you remain focused on the movement of your breath. Now, pause your inhalation for as long as possible at the base of your brain.

Finally, exhale completely out the top or crown of your head (*Sahasrara Chakra*).

Note that these instructions involve a visualization as do many of the Kriya Yoga instructions.

Feeble Breaths in the Third Eye (*Ajna Chakra*)

In this exercise, focus on the point between your eyebrows. Take such feeble breaths that your exhalations would not even fog a mirror held directly under your nostrils. Continue this exercise for 10 breaths.

It is important in this exercise to breathe deeply (not shallow), yet very softly, like the movement of a butterfly's wings when she sits on a flower petal. Remember, soft, slow, deep breaths.

Feeble Breaths in the Third Eye (*Sahasrara Chakra*)

In this exercise, focus on the crown of your head (*Sahasrara Chakra*), and take tiny feeble breaths into and out of your crown *chakra*. Take such feeble breaths that your exhalations would not even fog a mirror held directly under your nostrils. Continue this exercise for 10 breaths. It is important in this exercise to breathe deeply, yet very very softly.

So Ham Meditation

SO—HAM means "I am that"; "I am the same as the God Force". The ancient yogis, who spent years in utter meditative silence, heard the natural sound of the breath as *SO-HAM*. As you practice this meditation you affirm your oneness with your breath, and with the divine energy within you. This meditation can be practiced on its own, or at the end of the basic Kriya Yoga meditations described above.

Sit with your head, neck, and spine in vertical alignment. Touch the tips of your first finger and thumb. Breathe very slow *Ujjayi* breaths into your stomach, not your chest. With each incoming *Ujjayi* breath, silently recite the mantra SO in your mind. With each outgoing breath or exhalation, silently recite the mantra HAM.

Lesson 5

The Quantum God

The entire universe is made up of energy. Everything in this universe pulsates with the same subatomic energy; I like to call her *The God Force*.

When we break down any solid object into its smallest components, we find atoms and subatomic particles. Beyond the tiniest subatomic particles, physicists have discovered a powerful energy that is infinitely intelligent, self-aware, and radiates intense light. This energy is the God Force.

This energy gives life and animates humans, animals, plants, and even objects, like a rock. The subatomic God Force vibrates at very high frequencies, above one million cycles per second.

The laws of atomic physics teach us that the higher the vibrational frequency of an energy field, the more energetic that field is. For example, a cold frying pan exhibits less energy than a red hot frying pan. Although both frying pans are made of iron, the molecules within the cold frying pan are dense and move slowly, while the molecules of the red hot frying pan bounce about in a frenzy. What makes the molecules of the hot frying pan bounce around faster is heat. In spiritual terms, that heat is called *tapas* which literally means heat. As you continue your Kriya Yoga practices, you literally build up heat in your body and spinal column. This spiritual heat magnetizes and energizes your body so that the vibrational energy of your entire being increases.

Because the God Force vibrates at incredibly high frequencies, She has infinite power. High vibrating energy fields are invisible because they do not reflect light. Therefore, God is not visible to human eyes because of Her very high vibrational frequency. Highly energetic fields are very light, that is why the God Force can defy gravity. Also, high vibrating energy fields can penetrate and go through any solid barrier. This is why God can be everywhere, evenly present, at once.

Beyond the Speed of Light

Atomic physicists have found that beyond the speed of light, all ordinary laws of physics break down. Time and space bend and these two dimensions eventually disappear.

The God Force that is made of Pure Consciousness travels even faster than the speed of light. We, as human beings have access to this consciousness through subtle thought (when brain activity slows down). When our rambling thoughts cease and the mind becomes relatively still, we access Pure Consciousness in the gap between two thoughts. During such states, our mind becomes very self-aware and we gain awareness of our subtlest thoughts.

Our subtle thoughts travel even faster than the speed of light. This is why you can think of a friend and 5 minutes later they appear on the sidewalk in front of you, or you receive a long distance telephone call from that dear one way across two continents.

Beyond Time and Space

The God Force is beyond time. The God Force can simultaneously connect you to the past, present, and future. Many advanced yogis who are very high vibrating Beings, have the ability to see the past and the future, at once and accurately. Cosmic information related to various time periods is immediately available at the will of the Yogi.

The presence of the God Force is non-local—this means God is everywhere at once. Subatomic particles behave the same way; one electron can be located at two points simultaneously, without apparent travel through space.

Non-consensual

The experience of the God Force is non-consensual. This means you cannot look for other people's agreement or affirmation of your divine experiences. Everyone experiences the presence of God in a unique way. Other people's five senses cannot detect your intuitive contact with God.

Your Body—The House of God

Your own body is the house of God. You are made of cells, molecules, atoms, and subatomic particles. Beyond the smallest components of your body, the subatomic God Force (Pure Consciousness) pulsates and radiates light in your body. Halos and auras are not reserved for saints and prophets. Halos are radiations of the God Force vibrating at speeds in excess of one million cycles per second. Any high vibrating energy field generates light; what I am really saying is any human being who vibrates highly shines with a halo.

Despite our body being the house of God, most of us are not in touch with the God Force residing within. The reason most people are not in touch with the God Force is that their minds are very busy and their nervous systems have so many disturbances that hide the tiny, subtle vibrations of the God Force from ordinary awareness. In order for you to feel the very subtle, high vibrating God Force, you must be free of mental disturbances and mental chatter so that your awareness (inner radar) becomes very subtle and sensitive to the slightest movements of inner energy.

The God Force or Life Force vibrating in your body has many different names. She is referred to as *Prana* in Indian traditions, *Chi* and *Tao* in Chinese traditions, *Qi* in Japanese traditions, and *Holy Spirit* in Christian traditions. Whatever name you choose to associate with this divine presence within you, know that the energy remains the same.

The Self-Aware God Reflecting Back on Itself

The subatomic energy of God is self-aware; the God Force is composed of Pure Consciousness that is infinitely intelligent and self-aware. When you are thinking of God, God is aware that you are thinking of Her, the Creator. Putting it in another context, you are made of the God Force; when you are praying to God, the God Force of which you are composed is aware that you are praying to Her. I hope this is not too confusing, but when you pray, you are actually praying to your Self (Soul), and not any almighty power that is totally outside and separate of yourself. The true spiritual problem for most of us is that we refuse to imagine that the God Force also resides within our own cells, molecules, and atoms.

Consciousness, or the God Force, is an energy that is the cause of all material objects. Consciousness acts upon itself to remold itself into different creations. This divine energy turns inward on itself, looks back at Herself, and constantly changes and recreates Herself into multitudes of shapes and forms that our five human senses then perceive as visible matter within the material world. For example, spiritually speaking, a ballerina is actually the God Force wanting to experience Herself as a dancer.

The God Force responds to human consciousness and our subtlest thoughts. The outward results you achieve in your life depend on the questions you ask. Your predominant thoughts and fundamental beliefs shape all of your life results. Anything that is persistently in your mind, anything that you constantly think and concentrate on, manifests in your life because the subatomic God Force molds itself around your observations and beliefs. This is why many scriptures say, *you are what you think.*

Thus, this entire universe is just One energy reflecting back on itself.

The World Is, As You See It

As mentioned earlier, the God Force is aware of our consciousness and responds to our subtle intentions, manifesting what we focus on in our material world. This relationship between our subtle intentions and what manifests in the material world has been documented in science.

Physicists have discovered that there is a random probability of the electron appearing as a particle, then disappearing as an invisible energy wave. In fact, everything in this world exists in two forms: (1) invisible waves of energy (x-rays, radio waves); (2) visible solid, liquid, or gas.

What is astonishing is that physicists have discovered that the electron disappears into invisible waves of energy when humans are not observing it. Yet, when a human being conducts an experiment with the intention of observing an electron, the electron blinks into existence, in the form of a particle, with much greater probability than times when humans are not observing it! In simpler terms, what this means, is that whatever you choose to focus on, begins to manifest in your daily life.

Think about this for a moment; all external events and objects are composed of subatomic particles and atoms that respond to human beliefs and focused thought. In this same way, we create our own material reality through our subtle intentions and thought waves.

We create reality from the inside out. What appears in your life is what you want to see.

The Wave World and the Material World

Like the electron, everything in this universe has two aspects—invisible wave form and the less energetic solid form. We can only perceive one of these two aspects of reality at any one instant. What we usually perceive with our limited five senses is the solid and visible form of this world. Most of us are unable, with our five human senses, to perceive the underlying reality that is the subatomic wave world.

When you look at a beautiful piece of pottery, you may be fooled into thinking that the pot has its own existence. Yet, the master who makes hundreds of pots knows that all his masterpieces are made of that one essential substance--clay. In this example, it is the clay which is the subatomic God Force, the underlying cause of the beautiful pottery.

The enlightened Being, the one with the quiet mind, can perceive everything in both material form and wave form. This person has the ability to switch back and forth between the subatomic wave world and the solid material world.

The enlightened person knows that the underlying reality of life is One subatomic energy. She knows that cloud, water, and ice are all made of the same element (H_2O). The only difference between clouds and ice is the vibrational frequency or molecular motion; ice is denser and vibrates at a lower frequency than a path of cloud.

Knowing that clouds, water, and ice are all made of the same element is like having the spiritual knowledge that there is only One God Force or energy that animates everything in life.

Synchronicity

The relationship between your inner reality and its manifestation in the outer world is called synchronicity. The more in touch you are with your subatomic divine energy, the more external events reflect your inner consciousness, intentions, and thoughts.

For example, you will think of a friend and 5 minutes later they call you on the telephone. These events increase the more you deepen your meditation; because meditation increases your vibrational frequency enabling you to tune into the Creator which is ultimately responsible for all events in this world.

Synchronicity increases in your life as you make stronger and more regular connections with your God Force through meditation and other spiritual practices, like prayer. In other words, as your vibrational frequency increases, you witness plenty of incidents that are in harmony with what you have just been thinking and wishing.

Second Attention

In your daily life, focus your higher consciousness on the strange "coincidences" happening in your life. These are not coincidences; everything that happens in your life is a reflection of your inner state and your predominant thoughts and core beliefs. Your predominant thoughts program your subconscious mind and your subconscious mind creates the interplay between you and the subtle waves of the God Force.

As a spiritual practice, put part of your daily attention on the external events that "just happen". Ask yourself how these coincidences reflect your desires, intentions, intuitions, dreams, and your inner state.

Accessing the Quantum Source of Life

As mentioned earlier, everything in this world has two forms: a visible solid form and an invisible energy form. The Source of your life is your Spirit or the non-solid energy fields beyond your flesh and bones. Everything that you experience, yet cannot prove with your five senses, belongs to the wave world, the world of invisible energies. This includes spiritual experiences, love and other emotions, inspiration, creativity, intuition, déjà vu, dreams, etc.

The part of you that brings joy and life energy into you is your Spirit, your Soul. When we become too logical, rational, and intellectual our heart dries up because we lose contact with our Life Source (Spirit).

Do not ignore the mystical side of your life. Cherish and welcome deep emotions; dreams; hunches and intuitions; déjà vu experiences; meditation; prayer; conversations with little children, animals, and plants. These sides of your life are the richest sources of energy and joy; without them you will become depressed and dry.

Ignoring these parts of ourselves makes us lifeless and limits us to seeing only the solid, visible side of life in two dimensions instead of the unlimited dimensions of the wave world. The more open we are and the more interest we show in our own spiritual self, the more multidimensional and interesting life becomes.

The subatomic world of Spirit has no limitations. Anything is possible, because your own mind partners with the God Force and creates reality.

Manifesting Reality Through the Quantum Connection

Your seed thoughts or intentions are subtler and more refined than intellectual thoughts. Intellectual thought cannot co-create with

God; only subtle thoughts or Pure Consciousness can. In a state of non-thought, your subtle intentions stir the God Force and enable you to manifest reality.

Through our consciousness (subtle intention, <u>not intellect</u>) we participate in the creation and manifestation of material reality. To participate in the creation process with God, we need to transcend our body, intellectual mind, ego, and five senses—this occurs during states of deep relaxation, prayer, and meditation.

In a state of deep meditation and relaxation, our brain activity slows down from the busy Beta wave level to the Alpha, Theta, and Delta wave levels. Without the interference of brain activity (rambling thoughts), we are in full contact with Pure Consciousness—a state of non-thought coupled with a state of full awareness. In a state of non-thought, our awareness shifts from our solid form (body, mind, and senses) to our lighter outer layers, our Soul, vibrating at speeds equivalent to the God Force.

In a state of non-thought or relaxed awareness experienced during Alpha and Theta waves (refer to Lesson 15, The Mind), your deepest, most natural desires will manifest into reality; your intentions will influence the God Force.

Emptiness – The Source of Creativity

In the subatomic world, possibilities are endless because the quantum world is the Source of all creation.

Whenever you are stuck and have run out of ideas, empty your two-dimensional rational mind; the rational mind belongs to the limited material world.

Whenever you need a solution, the first step is to relax. Release your muscular tension with each exhalation and imagine that all your thoughts are flowing out of your nostrils leaving you serene and tranquil. Just relax into the moment and witness the play of life as if from the outside, like an onlooker.

Total relaxation increases your vibrational energy leading into the zone of silence, meditation, creative visualization, and Sixth Sense. Such states activate your Higher Mind which has access to creativity and solutions that lay beyond the reach of your rational mind.

The Key to Connecting with the Quantum God is Relaxation

To experience more dimensions of life and to access your higher mind, you need to relax your body and intellect (lower mind).

Those who experience God teach us to relax into the moment. The three key practices during meditation are: relax, witness the mind, and be lost in your object of meditation.

When you are looking for a solution, lie down on your back, consciously relax all your muscles, and stay conscious of your breathing. Meditate on your breath. Imagine that each exhalation expels all thoughts from your nostrils. Ride the movement of your exhalation to the depths of your Being.

Meditation—The Secret of Eternal Youth

Atomic physicists have also discovered that subatomic particles regenerate themselves much more quickly than the slower moving solid objects.

The less solid an energy field is, the quicker it can renew and regenerate itself. For example, a cloud can reshape and regenerate itself much quicker than a solid object such as an ice cube because the cloud molecules are moving much faster than the molecules within ice.

Humans age because they cannot regenerate new body cells as quickly as the old ones are dying. When you meditate and transcend your body, mind, and senses, the vibrational frequency of your body increases—you become less solid and more like the cloud. In that high frequency state, you can regenerate your body cells and renew your energy much more quickly. This increase in your vibrational frequency occurs in all states of deep relaxation such as meditation, deep prayer, breathing, yoga, and deep sleep.

Lesson 6

Space: The House of God

Ancient mystics believed that the space you are surrounded with is not dead, rather buzzing with an intelligent God Force.

How blissful you would feel if you knew that the space that surrounds you and the whole universe was alive and divine. Afterall, everything in this universe exists within space. The only thing that was never invented and that has always existed is space. Space even existed before the Big Bang. The one dimension that cradles our galaxy and all others is space. Would you ever feel lonely again if you knew that the space that embraces your body were alive and divine?

All solid matter that you see before your eyes is mostly empty space. This is because solid matter is made of atoms and the atom itself is empty. Scientists say that the relative distance between the electron and the nucleus of the atom (neutron) is the same as the distance between the earth and the moon. Given that the atom is so tiny that six million sit on the tip of a needle – that is a lot of space!

The same vast emptiness that exists inside the atom also exists in your body. It looks like our bodies are solid, but in actuality, we are made of cells, which are in turn composed of molecules, and molecules themselves are made of empty atoms. If the space within the atom were pulsating with intelligence and divinity, wouldn't you be the embodiment of God?

Connecting with the God Force

It might seem that we cannot directly experience the vast void of space because space, where God lives, is emptiness or nothingness and we cannot intellectually study "nothingness." However, we can experience nothingness by withdrawing our five senses from the objects of the outer world and focusing them on the inner world — the empty space between two thoughts or two breaths is nothingness.

If we withdraw our senses from external objects and put our awareness on the space around us (emptiness), we experience a shift in consciousness. We feel light, joyful, and clear-minded because we are now focused on God pulsating in space. This is what we do during meditation; we empty ourselves, withdraw our five senses away from external objects and collect our senses within ourselves.

During waking or working hours, the equivalent of space-awareness is staying in the present moment. Stay present and check in regularly with your inner body and the movements of your breath. You will feel lightness, joy, and clarity as you return to the present moment.

Emptiness Meditation

Lie on your back. Breathe into your stomach. Tense and relax different parts of your body — legs, stomach, arms, hands, throat, face. After the tension/relaxation exercise, stay lying on your back, on the floor; place your awareness on different points in the body. When you place your awareness on a certain body part, you will automatically breathe *Prana* (Life Force) into this part of the body.

During the same meditation, while taking your breath and attention to different body parts, also notice any physical sensations in these body parts. Be aware of the air coming into your body. The in-breath energizes and vitalizes while the out-breath relaxes and releases tension. Feel Prana fill each body part with each inhalation; consciously relax each body part with each exhalation. You can also release mental chatter with each exhalation.

Continue taking deep breaths into your stomach while focusing your attention on different body parts and imagining the breath coming in and out of those body parts. As you breathe into the various parts of the body, visualize each specific body part dissolving into emptiness with the motion of the exhalation.

An example of part of the sequence:
Place your attention on the tip of your nose. Focus on your breath as it comes into and goes out of the tip of your nose. Continue taking deep breaths while focusing on the flow of air in and out of your nostrils. Now, with each exhalation, imagine the tip of your nose gradually dissolving into emptiness.

Now, shift your awareness to your throat and breathe into your throat. Follow your breath as you visualize that with each exhalation the passageway between your nose and throat dissolves into emptiness.

Keep following your breath as it moves from your throat to the point between your eyebrows. Follow your breath at the point between your eyebrows. Keep following your breath within the Third Eye with intense awareness. With each exhalation, imagine that your Third Eye dissolves into light and emptiness.

Next, place your attention on your heart. Breathe into your heart. Feel your heart expand with each inhalation, and with each exhalation, imagine that your heart dissolves into light and emptiness.

Be aware of your stomach. The air comes into your stomach and flows out of your stomach. With each exhalation, imagine your stomach dissolving into light and emptiness.

Bring your focus and breath into both legs and feel the air filling both of your legs with life and energy. With each exhalation, imagine your legs dissolving into light and emptiness.

Bring your attention and breath into your feet. Follow your breath from your feet up to the fontanel at the top-center of your head. As your breath passes through the length of your body imagine with each exhalation your entire body dissolving into light and emptiness.

Now focus on the space outside your body. With each exhalation, imagine that you are moving outward and merging with empty space. Rest in that space like a Spirit or Witness.

Now, take very feeble breaths into the fontane and let your breath take you beyond the top of your head, into the sky.

With each exhalation, you and all of space dissolve into light and emptiness.

Lesson 7

The Laws of Effortless Action in the Material World

As meditation deepens, it feels as though the color of the lenses through which we look at life change. Though we live in the same world, through higher levels of consciousness we literally experience a different reality (deeper and clearer) within the same environment.

Though meditation has a big role in this transformation, the grace of the *Guru* is also critical to the seeker's transformation. The *Guru* has very high currents of spiritual electricity running through his or her body; this spiritual electricity is called *the Guru Principle* or *Grace*. When the *Guru* enters the seeker's life, grace literally surrounds them. Suddenly, the seeker enjoys full cooperation of natural forces; windows of opportunity open up everywhere; and greater levels of success are achieved through lesser amounts of effort. Life will no longer be such a struggle.

As levels of consciousness change due to grace and deepening of meditation, seekers experience life differently. It can be said that seekers who enter the inner journey of meditation and other practices experience three different states of consciousness. Each time our level of consciousness changes, it is as if the lens through which we are viewing life changes colors. A change in the stage of consciousness may feel very confusing to a seeker; the presence of a *Guru* or wise Guide is very critical since that sage can explain, based on direct experience, exactly what the seeker is experiencing and why.

The Three Stages of Consciousness

1. Transcendent Consciousness

This is the state of deep calm and restful awareness correlating with deep meditation. This state corresponds to Alpha brain waves which measure approximately 7 cycles per second. In the beginning of our meditative practice we only experience transcendent consciousness during silent meditation sessions. In this stage of consciousness you are either transcending body, mind, and senses, or you are totally involved and entangled in external activity through your body, mind, and senses. The two states of calm witnessing (transcendence) and entanglement cannot co-exist during this stage of consciousness. Rest and tranquility only exist during formal meditation sittings not during activity.

2. Cosmic Consciousness

After a longer period of regular meditation, a deeper sense of calm and restful awareness develops. In the state of Cosmic Consciousness it is possible to walk into any activity while maintaining a state of inner silence and establishment in your inner Being. In this stage of consciousness, which corresponds to Theta brain waves measuring approximately 3.5 cycles per second, you experience your real Self (your Soul) as a separate witness of daily activity. You are fully engaged in life, but not attached to the activity or its outcome. In this phase, you always experience your inner silence (your Soul) while engaged in activity. It is as if you walk into any worldly activity while surrounded by a bubble of inner silence.

The big difference between Cosmic Consciousness and Transcendent Consciousness is the potential for full awareness of activity and simultaneous immersion in your silent Self. In Cosmic Consciousness, you do not need to be in deep meditation to detach from daily activities and their end-results, this happens spontaneously and effortlessly.

3. *God Consciousness*

Finally, as you maintain regular contact with your inner God your entire life becomes an act of worship. During the first two phases you experience God inside yourself. In this final stage the God Force acts directly through you permeating every aspect of your life. Every one of your thoughts, words, and actions are acts of divinity and in complete harmony with natural laws. While witnessing all the diversity of the external world you experience only One God Force (subatomic wave) pulsating in everything.

Complete Knowledge

Complete knowledge is comprised of both intellectual understanding and direct contact with our Soul (*Atman*).

We gain understanding by studying scriptures, literature, and talks by enlightened sages. We gain direct experience of our own divinity through deep relaxation and meditation.

Only the combination of spiritual study and meditation will bring about higher-consciousness. Given the choice between silent practice and intellectual study, always give top priority to your silent practice since more than 70 percent of spiritual progress comes through direct experience of your inner God (Soul), not intellectual understanding of enlightened words.

Action is Required

To reach higher states of consciousness, you absolutely must act toward that direction. Action is necessary in life; the laws of nature require that we take action. Non-action is impossible for any Being in this universe; if you do not take action, you will wither and die. Even those who have dedicated their lives to the pursuit of truth and meditation are constantly involved in inner action. Meditation itself is a purposeful action. Do not think that the true sage or *Guru* merely sits all day chanting *AUM*; the enlightened ones are very involved in social reform and services.

Every one of your thoughts, emotions, words, and actions create waves that influence the atmosphere around you. These waves travel through space and impact your environment. Every time your individual thought waves collide with the God Force the energy of your thoughts boomerang back to you. The boomerang effect is nature's reaction to your original action. Thus, the God Force simply mirrors your energy right back to you. Be careful what you think and make sure you take full responsibility for the consequences of your thoughts, words, and actions. Only when you accept full responsibility for these consequences do you evolve into a spiritually mature individual.

Three Kinds of Action

There are three kinds of action:

- Mental (intentions and thoughts)

- Verbal (words and sentences)

- Physical (outward actions and reactions)

Of the three kinds of action, intentions and thoughts (mental actions) are the most powerful because they have the highest vibrational energy. Your verbal actions (speech) are, in turn, more powerful than physical actions because words coming through your vocal cords vibrate at a higher frequency than your physical actions.

The mind is everything. It is our most powerful instrument. The mind's intentions influence the power of our words and actions. The power of our words and physical actions depend totally on the mental intention behind our words and actions. For example, either a doctor or a criminal can cut your body with a knife, but the intention behind the knife wound is very different. The cut of a surgeon has a healing effect as compared to the stab of a criminal energized with the intention to kill.

The Quality of Your Actions

Students always ask *how can I think, speak, and act like an enlightened sage?* The quality of your thoughts, words, and actions depend on the level of your consciousness.

As your meditation and your contact with the highest Self become stronger your thoughts, words, and actions naturally maximize your own wellbeing as well as that of society.

Your Actions Are In the Service of the God Force

At the highest levels of consciousness you become one with natural laws, and you become an instrument of the God Force. All of your guidance comes from God and natural laws, and all of your actions become spontaneously life supporting.

In Cosmic Consciousness, you perform actions as an individual. In God Consciousness, even your inactivity produces divine waves of energy at the level of creation.

Consequences of Your Actions

The seed of each action is your intention and the quality of thought behind that action. If you perform actions with intentions that are harmful to yourself and society, you will later suffer the consequences. There is really no way to reverse the bad consequences (*karma*) of actions and words that arise from harmful intentions.

There is an important issue to understand in relation to consequences of your actions; if a person who has studied and practiced spiritual concepts breaks the spiritual laws of nature despite his profound understanding, he will suffer much stronger negative *karma* as compared to a fool who has no understanding of God, love, or natural laws. The God Force expects wise people to teach the world by living truly human values.

Non-Attachment to Desires and Results

With continued meditation, our mind and our awareness become increasingly subtle. When the first thought of action occurs we identify intentions and desires underlying the action. Because we catch our intentions and desires right at the seed level, we release our attachment to desires and results before we even begin acting on them.

Those who are anchored in their inner silence perform action without being attached to the result of the action.

Tireless Action

As a general rule of thumb, deep mental and emotional impressions make us very tired during and after activity. The reason we become fatigued during activity is because the activity and the objects we are involved with leave impressions on the surface of our minds. You can think of the mind as a CD, and each activity may leave an impression (a scratch) on the surface of the conscious or the subconscious mind. These impressions eventually turn into a storehouse of our past experiences; the negative past impressions can impact our present behavior in a negative way because we are juxtaposing our past onto this present moment.

When you become established in your inner silence through deep meditation, activity and external circumstances no longer leave deep or lasting impressions on your mind. You will perform action and let go of the results with a sense of freedom and lightness. The only experience that leaves a lasting impression on the mind of a meditator is the experience of direct contact with the Soul.

Maintaining one's self while involved in action requires direct experience of one's Soul (Pure Consciousness). This quality of detachment from one's activity cannot be understood intellectually. Such detachment increases as you progress through the daily practice of meditation.

Following Our Own Path

Each person has come to this life with a unique path and mission. This destiny, called *dharma* in Sanskrit, is your calling and is based on your natural God-given talents.

When we envy someone else and try to duplicate their *dharma* we lose our own natural balance. By envying someone else we allow their consciousness to invade our consciousness. Be careful because envy has a very draining and destructive effect on your Soul. Be true to your Self and follow your own path!

Self-Control

There are some traditions that emphasize self-control as a means of raising consciousness. This approach is frustrating and will ultimately not work.

When you transcend your intellectual mind, body, and five senses during meditation you come into contact with Pure Consciousness (your Soul). As you become established in the sweet silence of your Soul, your five senses turn inward and tap into their highest Source of contentment and joy (the Soul). Once your senses have tasted the rich inner life they understand where "home" is. With this deeper connection many shallow forms of "fun" lose their attraction. Nothing compares to the richness of inner contentment. Therefore, if you simply meditate and continue your spiritual practices, this sense of richness will satisfy you to the degree that you will not have to forcefully discipline yourself to stay away from external fun.

When you turn the mind inward, the senses follow the mind. Self-control will automatically come. Your senses always follow your mind. The mind is the commander-in-chief of the five senses. When the mind becomes more settled by following the motion of the breath inward, your senses will also turn inward and lose much of their addictions and craving for instant external gratification. The self-control you need will automatically come—you do not have to struggle for self-control at the personality level.

The Daily Life of a Realized Person

The enlightened person's life is comprised of an inward cycle (meditation) followed by an outward cycle (activity).

Go into meditation, receive guidance and energy from your Soul, then come out and materialize what you gained in meditation in the material world.

Here is the formula for success:

> Think
> Act
> Think
> Act

Each 20-minute meditation establishes you in your inner silence.

This inner silence arising from a 20-minute meditation, can last through about 10 hours of activity. After this amount of activity the effects of the prior meditation begin to fade. You can recharge yourself through a second evening meditation.

As you continue meditating for years, external activity no longer overshadows your inner sense of tranquility and centeredness (Soul). In higher states of consciousness, you do not need to meditate as much to maintain your sense of centeredness.

Faith

Faith is a critical component of effortless action and spiritual growth. However, it is not required at the time you begin spiritual practice. Anyone at any level of faith can begin meditating. Once you experience transcending your body, intellectual mind, and five senses your faith will deepen.

The biggest cause for lack of faith is not having direct experience of inner silence. Once you contact your inner depths, even for a second, you never forget this experience and your faith automatically strengthens.

There are three kinds of faith:

Faith in Yourself

Although at first you do not believe or experience this, ultimately, you are God. Faith in yourself is a private and deep belief that you are made in the image of God, that you are worthy, and that you are most powerful when you are aligned with your highest truth.

Faith in the Guru

Find a Guide whom you intuitively trust. Follow the teachings of this *Guru* for as long as her teachings invigorate you, for as long as her teachings resonate with your inner truth. Doubt in your Guide and you will delay or destroy your spiritual progress.

When a spiritual seeker is progressing from Transcendental Consciousness to Cosmic Consciousness, and finally God Consciousness, this person's perceptions of the life events change from one stage of consciousness to another. This is like first looking through green-colored sunglasses then switching to brown-colored sunglasses.

If the guidance of a *Guru* is not available, changes in consciousness may confuse and even discourage a student from continuing. In the absence of a realized *Guru*, a student undergoing a major change in consciousness may think he is going mad.

Faith in one's Self and one's Guru is very important because it helps the seeker maintain and build courage while continuing toward another unknown state of consciousness.

Faith in God

Once you experience your inner God (*Shakti*) during meditation, you will develop faith in the existence of a subatomic, self-aware Creative Force vibrating in you and in all of the universe. The Life Force is full of love and will be your ultimate protector as you establish daily contact with Her.

Lesson 8

Life as a Mirror

God, and the world that God created, is a mirror that reflect your inner state. Whatever you experience in the outer world is a result of your predominant thoughts and core beliefs. This is why so many scriptures insist *you are what you think.*

The subatomic God Force is fluid energy. This divine energy turns inward on itself, looks back at itself, and constantly changes and recreates itself into multitudes of shapes and forms that our five senses perceive as the material world. Moreover, quantum physicists have also discovered that the subatomic God Force also mirrors or mimics human thoughts and intentions.

Quantum physics laboratories are now discovering that the results of quantum experiments are dependent on the consciousness and expectations of the scientist conducting that experiment. In other words, the subatomic Creator (God Force) mirrors our own intentions and predominant beliefs back to us by constructing a material reality that reflects our recurring thoughts and beliefs. The energy we transmit outward as our beliefs and intentions influence the God Force which then manifests the very same results in our external life.

Everything you think about, your words, and your actions radiate outwards like waves and are mirrored back to you in the form of identical reactions from nature. Think about these examples:

If you are angry, life will show you anger.

If you are aloof and secluded, people will not approach you or will shut you out.

If you judge people, others will also judge you.

If you are fearful, everyone around will pick up on your fear and return scary circumstances back to you.

If you love yourself, loving people will surround you.

In other words, you create all of your external life circumstances through your beliefs and mental habits — *we create all our life experiences from inside out.*

How to Break Patterns that Make Life Difficult

When you experience difficulty in your life, go within and ask yourself why this pain exists in your life. Ask your Soul, *which aspect of me is the God Force mirroring back to me?* When you experience joy, know that you have created love and joy. Again, look inside and identify the beautiful energy within that has reflected love and joy back into your life.

Friends and Life-Partners as Teachers

Your life-partner, lover, or friends are in relationship with you so you can learn important spiritual lessons from them. Each partner has characteristics that push the other partner's "buttons" so that your ego will be challenged and you can grow beyond your present mental concepts and limitations.

For instance, if you are jealous and your mate is flirtatious in a way that arouses your jealousy, then you learn a lesson about jealousy. Chances are your life-partner has been placed in your life by the God Force to teach you an important spiritual lesson — to release your false jealousy.

The God Force is providing an opportunity for you to be free from this negativity so you can proceed with your spiritual growth.

How the God Force Teaches Us Lessons

God is not cruel; She is a quiet, humble mirror who teaches you by mirroring your own energy back to you. When you are feeling challenged, look inside and you will discover the particular negative energy you are broadcasting outward. When you change your intention, attitude, and old thought patterns, suddenly the world will respond differently to you.

You may be amazed by the simplicity and depth of this statement:

To change your life all you have to do is change your thoughts and beliefs.

When your beliefs change, your actions change; when your actions change, your life results change.

Exercise – How Nature Mirrors Your Energy Back to You

Keep a notebook and list your thoughts, emotions, and actions for a few days. Opposite to the column listing each thought, emotion, or action keep track of nature's (other people or the environment's) response to your actions and how nature mirrors your own energy back to you.

You should find that whatever energy you put out toward your environment through your thoughts, words, and actions comes back to you like a boomerang. You should notice this is equally true for both positive and negative energy. The God Force does not really care what energy you put out there; She simply mirrors your energy back to you.

Lesson 9

Relationships

Think about the relatedness of our universe:

1. Rain falls on an apple tree
2. The apple tree blossoms
3. Bees drink from the apple blossoms and make honey
4. We eat the honey, grow strong, and eventually grow old and die
5. Our bodies become fertile earth
6. Rain falls on the earth
7. Vapor from the trees and earth make clouds
8. Clouds make rain
9. Rain falls on the apple tree

Do you see how everything in this universe is a cycle of giving and receiving?

There is no way to be out of relationships. We are all in relationships all of the time. The only part of nature that thinks in selfish terms of isolation is the human ego — the feeling of "I-ness."

Our Primary Relationship—the Soul

Our first relationship is with our Self. If you learn to love your inner Self (God incarnated in you), you will be naturally filled with love; love is the quality of Soul-consciousness. A direct relationship with your Soul and the God Force requires that you be able to tune into or resonate with high vibrations associated with the Soul (above 200,000 cycles per second). Deep meditation allows you to tune into your higher and divine energy layers. When you are tuned into these non-solid layers during deep meditation, you begin to vibrate highly. When you truly love yourself as God, others will benefit from divine, loving vibrations emanating from you.

When you are in love with the Self, you can fully love others. Therefore, the ultimate relationship for each of us is with our Self.

An important spiritual practice is to take your focus off others once or twice a day, and cast your gaze inwards. During this exercise, you can meditate on *breath coming in/breath going out.* Nurture your private life: go out to nature; meditate; learn to enjoy *sweet solitude;* read and contemplate spiritual literature; take long walks; participate in creative activities such as dance, painting, sculpture, writing, etc. These activities are very nurturing to the Soul. The deepest intimacy comes from going within. The richest source of joy, love, security, and peace comes from your inner Being. Ultimately, the wise person looks for inner contentment which then overflows in the form of joy and contentment into their outer life. The other unending source of contentment is giving and receiving love. You will see that the satisfaction coming from love always outlasts material possession.

When you come to know your inner Self, you realize it is the same Self (energy of consciousness) that resides in everyone and everything else. There is only One God Force and She resides everywhere, even in empty space.

Relationships Are an Exchange of Subtle Energy

What is really exchanged in a relationship is energy, not the give and take witnessed through the five senses on the physical plane. The five senses always place emphasis on the exchange of thoughts, words and actions; however the real exchange that occurs in any human interaction is the exchange of subtle invisible energies. Whatever seems to be happening on the physical level is simply a result of underlying subtle energies being exchanged.

Relationships Are Constantly Changing

The law of this universe is constant change. Therefore relationships are also ever-changing. We cannot grab on to a relationship and hold on to it in a fixed position. Relationships are fluid and dynamic. If we let go of fear, we will look at our relationships as daily adventures into the unknown. If we maintain inner-honesty and let our relationships evolve in any direction that naturally comes, we will make great spiritual progress.

When it comes to relationships, the highest truth is to maintain inner honesty. Approach the other person with the purest love and highest level of honesty that you can gather. Know that if you fear and resist change, your relationships will not last. Any relationship will dry up and die if you try to resist its constant change.

Egocentric Love

The ego-centered person will only love others as long as these "others" fulfill their needs. Egocentric relationships are founded on the question *what's in it for me?*

In egocentric relationships, if someone does not fulfill our expectations, we may suddenly fall "out of love". The minute your partner stops quenching your inner thirst, your partner changes from a lover to an opponent. You may experience feelings of anger, jealousy, hatred, regret, etc.

This is the quality of egocentric love. Egocentric love is based on dependencies instead of inner contentment.

Lack of Inner Completeness Is Not Love

Most relationships today are based on insecurity; they are a form of addiction. People tend to choose partners out of a deep-seated sense of fear, insecurity, emptiness, lack, and incompleteness.

It is common to confuse this lack of inner completeness with love. Ego-based attachment, the sense of addiction to any partner is in reality a way of using someone else to cover up our inner pain; our lack of contact with our Soul.

The truth is that you cannot "get" anything from anyone else in a relationship. When we take our focus off our own inner God (Self) we lose contact with our source of happiness and security. This is how we become addicted to others and why we seek to fill ourselves with someone else's energy. True contentment can never come from someone else; we must fill our own cup by making contact with our inner Self.

When we are overflowing with self-love, we have a sense of inner completeness. We can then share that love with a loved one. Love that flows from self-love is the only kind that lasts.

Love Is Internal Not External

In an insecure egocentric relationship, sexual union is an effort to gain wholeness, but even sexual ecstasy is temporary because we are not centered in our own Soul. Nothing or no one external can put you in contact with your truest Self. This is your spiritual work. Meditate and follow the truth of your heart.

As long as we are identified with our minds and external sources for our identification, we feel insecure and conduct our relationships based on insecurity.

Through continued meditation, the ego becomes much smaller and becomes integrated with the Self (Soul). When you contact your Soul and your ego shrinks, you will love others unconditionally, without expectations. You will not judge yourself or others; you will love yourself and others unconditionally.

Think how much happier your lover, your husband, your children would be if you unconditionally loved them for who they really were, instead of loving them on the condition that they obey your wishes and expectations.

Human Attractions

Human Beings are dynamic electromagnetic fields. Energy Field Theory proves that complementary fields are attracted to one another and non-complementary fields repel each other. So it is with people — some attract each other and others repel one another.

Energy Field Theory further explains that weaker energy fields are attracted to stronger ones so that the weaker field can revitalize itself. So it is with human interactions — have you noticed how people gather around a charismatic leader like a flock of bees thirsty for honey?

Meditation increases your vibrational frequency, thereby changing the quality of your energy field. When you change your "vibes", all of your tastes, habits, and relationships also change. When you release some of your old negative mental habits and old emotional baggage, your energy field strengthens and you begin to attract more positive people into your life.

True inner beauty comes through meditation and contact with your highest Self (Soul). It is not your education, your clothes, your car, or your money that truly impresses other people. In the final analysis, it is your inner state and your energy field that influence how others respond to you. When you feel inner beauty and love, you become irresistible to others.

Students often ask this question, *I am feeling very good and content, but I have someone in my private life that is draining my energy—what can I do?* Meditation will strengthen your energy field. With a strong energy field, you can filter negative influences of all kinds.

Relationships Mirror Your Inner State

Relationships are mirrors of our own internal state. We attract others based on our own beliefs and based on our qualities. You cannot possibly attract anyone unless they somehow complement your beliefs or personal qualities. For example, if all your friends are undependable, you need to look within and understand how you yourself are unreliable.

What you dislike in others is always what you dislike or cannot accept about yourself. Ask yourself if you are willing to give up your own negativities. Once you drop your negative and self-defeating beliefs, people who originally came to you based on your negative self images and beliefs will either change or leave your life. Take the example of a little girl who watched her mother being physically abused by Dad. This little girl is now a young woman in her third abusive relationship being beaten by one violent man after another. Once this woman identifies her old belief that women are to be abused, and once she releases such self-destructive beliefs, almost instantly abusive men will cease walking into her life.

With continued meditation and the changing of your energy field, friends who have been draining and depleting you, will lose interest in the empowered you. An entirely new social circle with vibrations harmonious to yours will form around you.

Being Open to Love

I have met people who are always hunting and searching for love. Never be thirsty for love; do not search for love. When you let go of your search, love comes to you. People who desperately seek love actually repel their potential mates. Remember, the God Force reflects your own desperate thoughts and obsessions right back to you. When you hunt for love, you are giving the universe the message; *I am hungry and deprived for love.* When the God Force hears your desperate message, She simply mirrors the same result back to you — *yes, you are right, you are indeed desperate and lacking in love.*

To erase your negative thoughts about lack of love, mentally repeat these affirmations all day:

> *My life is full of love.*

> *I accept love into my life, now.*

> *My friends and family adore me.*

> *I deserve plenty of love in my life.*

Falling In Love

The experience of falling in love is actually the Universe mirroring the beauty of your own Soul back to you. When you gaze into a lover's eyes, you actually adore the beautiful reflection of your own Self in your lover's eyes.

Marriage Is an Interdependent Relationship

A marital union, like all of nature, is an interdependent relationship. There is really no room for egoism and selfishness in marriage. Marriage really means the absolute sharing of your lives with each other.

A Healthy Marriage and Family Life

I truly believe that behind every successful person lies a loving and supportive mate and family. As humans we need to feel unconditional love; we need to know that someone believes in us deeply, even during moments when we do not believe in ourselves.

Here are some suggestions that may help you develop and maintain a healthy marriage and family life:

Develop a Long-Term Vision

The survival of a marriage and family requires a long-term perspective. The really high rates of divorce today are based on a short-term perspective, even the total absence of a vision regarding the meaning of marriage and family life. When a couple mutually believes in a long-term vision and commitment, the shorter-term challenges and difficult cycles do not throw that family off balance.

Develop Trust

Ninety percent of the energy exchange between humans is emotional energy. Love-based trust is a very empowering emotion. When we work hard to develop trust amongst family members, our interactions become so much easier because we do not always have to explain ourselves to suspicious family members who have been disappointed or hurt on prior occasions. It takes so much less energy to share a life in an environment of trust.

An example of how a lack of trust adversely affects a marriage: I have had students who come for spiritual counseling—the wife thinks the husband is cheating on her so she goes out and buys telephone spying equipment. After 6 months of spying on her husband's telephone calls, the wife is a nervous disaster and filled with anger, self-pity, and confusion. When you suspiciously spy on your mate you are assuming that you are replaceable and worthless, and therefore, you are deeply insulting your own Soul. If someone turns their back on your love, value yourself, and let them leave.

Remain Very Honest With One Anothe, and Keep Your Promises

Honorable people are those who are very honest, most importantly with themselves, and of course, with their family members. Deep honesty requires that we constantly listen to the voice of our conscience. When we treat our spouse and family members with integrity and honesty they develop a deep trust in us. This honesty and trust become the unchanging principle of the family interactions.

Practice Effective Communication

Effective communication means mutual understanding. Take time to really listen to your partner. Put yourself in the place of your spouse when difficulties arise; always first examine your own role in creating the problem before blaming others. Listen with empathy and acknowledge the other's feelings.

Realize the Notion of a "Perfect Romance" Is a Myth

Understand that marriage requires regular upkeep and maintenance. Even the most romantic lovers can fall out of love if they do not do the work required to nurture the relationship. Do not shy away from painful periods in your marriage; have the courage to speak to each other regarding expectations and disappointments.

Accept and Support Change and Growth Among Family Members

Although most of us are uncomfortable with change, the reality is that relationships are always changing; if you do not accommodate the changes that your partner and other family members are undergoing, your relationships will deteriorate.

Role Modeling Is Extremely Important

More than 90 percent of how you influence your children is through modeling — how you actually live out your own life in front of your kids, without sermoning. Your children's lives are actually shaped by the values and lifestyle that you live out on a daily basis.

All of your advice and your words have less than 10 percent impact on your children! What I am saying is live the values that you are preaching to your children; if you do not *walk your talk*, you will lose credibility as a parent and your words will have no effect on your children. When your children grow up, their adult lives will mirror the values that you actually modeled during their childhood.

Maintain a Balance Between Independence and Interdependence

As I mentioned in the beginning of this lesson, your first relationship is with your Self. If you do not love yourself, you cannot love anyone. First, deepen your relationship with yourself. It is okay to take time for yourself in a marital relationship and family life. Do not negate nurturing your private life. Meditate; spend time in nature; take long walks; learn to enjoy *sweet solitude*; read and contemplate spiritual literature; get involved in a creative activity such as dance, painting, sculpture, writing, etc.

Once you come to know and love your Self, then, learn to live interdependently with your family members. In an unhealthy family, several individuals live under the same roof, and there is interdependency, that is, there are no healthy personal boundaries between family members—you do not know where the mother ends and where the child begins. This kind of enmeshment creates many emotional dysfunctions. It is good for family members to trust and nurture each other, but each family member should learn how to nurture his or her own Soul, body, and mind. Healthy individuals and families have strong relationships with their inner selves, and they maintain healthy boundaries while providing loving support.

Engage in Public Service

Involve your entire family in some sort of public service. I mean unconditional service to society without expecting recognition or a reward. This kind of unconditional service brings deep peace to each individual as well as a powerful energy that protects your entire family.

Come to a Mutual Understanding Regarding Priorities

Functional families have come to a common understanding regarding their life priorities. You can even write a joint family letter outlining what all family members agree on in terms of what is the most important priority within that family.

Develop Internal Security

A family's sense of security should come from internal sources such as love, meditation, personal health, personal recreation time, unconditional love for the Self and other family members. If family members deeply believe in each other, that will be the greatest source of confidence and security for all the family members.

Changing Others

In the history of humankind, no one has ever changed another person. Others change only when they are ready and no longer resistant to change. It is like quitting smoking; you can try all sorts of gimmicks, but you will only quit smoking when you are really sick and tired of smoking. That point of releasing one's resistance is a holy junction.

Do not struggle trying to change others. Instead of trying to change others, look within and change yourself. When you change yourself, others around you will also pick up on your good energy and will naturally be healed in your light and love.

How to Help the One(s) You Love

Happiness is a personal and intentional decision. Therefore, you can never bring true lasting happiness to other people. They must do their own inner work and realize their own truth.

The best way to care for and be concerned with others is through service, empathy, kindness, and compassion. The wrong way to care about your beloved is to forget your inner Self. It is essential to love your Self in order to recharge your own energy system. Your job is to work on contacting your own inner Self and finding your own source of joy and contentment. Only then can you love others without conditions and judgment.

When you are filled with the love of your Soul, you can stand aside and love others unconditionally. With the strength and confidence that you gain from Self love you can support others in their pursuit of truth. When you are content and your cup is overflowing, you can give a lot more to others.

Remember, no person can be dependent on anyone else for the Life

Force (ultimate happiness). You are also not responsible for other people's emotions, nor are you responsible for fixing or healing anyone else. Everyone must learn their own highest truth.

Ultimately, everyone must be willing to accept help before they can be helped. When you see someone close to you is ready to change and grow, you can simply be there for them, love them, and watch as they Self-actualize.

The End of Relationships

We are most attracted (sexually or as friends) to those that most strongly mirror our highest spiritual lessons and truths.

On the physical plane, we will stay in relationships for as long as we need to learn our most important spiritual lessons. Once we learn these lessons, this relationship will either continue to teach us more, and we maintain our spiritual connection with each other, or we move on to another relationship that teaches us higher lessons in life. Spiritually speaking, a relationship that no longer supports your growth is dead — in this case, the marriage document is just collecting dust in a drawer.

Being Selective About Your Relationships

All of our thoughts, words, and actions vibrate outward and impact those around us. You are also subject to the vibrational frequency of others. Therefore, be selective about who you associate with. Avoid those people who deplete your energy. Of course, the stronger your own energy field is, the less other people will affect you. Your strong energy field acts as a filter to block out unwanted negativity.

Many of the scriptures remind us that the fastest way to enlightenment is keeping the company of the wise and the loving.

Lesson 10

Understanding Our Emotions

Emotions are fleeting impulses of energy; they are currents of spiritual electricity that run through us. Energy aroused is what we experience as emotion. Thus, emotions are *energy in motion* within our body.

Emotional energy continuously arises from one of our seven energy centers (*chakras)* and radiates outward to our cells and molecules. Physically, we feel our emotions mostly in the vicinity of our major energy centers.

Emotions Directly Impact Our Physical Body

Western scientists have recently discovered that every emotion generates a specific kind of amino acid called neuropeptides. This form of protein, specific to each kind of emotion, lodges itself against the cell walls and begins to change the internal structure of our cells. Therefore, every emotion directly impacts our physical body through the related proteins that impact our cells. After a while, our body cells can become addicted to each emotional protein. For example, a person who often feels guilt actually develops an addiction to the emotion of guilt because her cells have become addicted to the specific protein related to the emotion of guilt.

Relation of Emotions to Physical Sensations and Thoughts

Emotional intelligence means knowing what you and others are feeling at any given moment. This requires practice and stillness of mind because subtle and momentary emotions are hard to perceive and often escape our awareness. People who have inner awareness and emotional intelligence know that every emotion has a corresponding physical sensation in the body as well as an accompanying thought. Thus, every emotion has the following components:

- Mental (thought)
- Emotional
- Physical

We feel the physical component of emotions in the form of a physical sensation in the body and changes in our breathing. The mental component of emotion is in the form of a thought wave that gives rise to that particular emotion in the first place.

Each person's emotions, corresponding physical sensations, and thoughts are unique to that individual.

Emotions as Impermanent Waves of Energy

It is an illusion when we treat fleeting emotions as permanent states of our Being. If you meditate on the inner physical sensations of your body, on your emotions and thoughts, you will see that a permanent state of "I" does not exist. You are simply a fluid energy field made of impermanent waves of energy that come out of nothingness (pure Being) and dissipate back into nothingness.

Negative emotions are like clouds that temporarily block the sun. Always remember that emotions are temporary and passing. Your authentic Being is like the unchanging sky in the background. With proper understanding of emotions as impermanent waves of energy, you will have confidence when overcome with a powerful emotion that *this too will soon pass.*

Exercise – Feeling Emotions in Our Body

When powerful emotions overtake you, breathe deep, feel the physical location of the emotion in your body; sense its movement and quality. Relax your mind and body in order to fully experience and witness the emotion and its physical and mental counterparts. By witnessing the emotion you allow it to pass through you and resist clinging to it as if the emotion were a lasting reality. You simply witness these phenomena without being identified or entangled.

Understanding the Root of Emotions—the Inward Gaze

Most people think that changing a job, a home, or car will change their emotions. This is a misconception; a job, home and car are superficial appearances. You need to understand the internal root of your emotions. Understand that changing your external circumstances or the people in your life will not transform you emotionally. Instead of criticizing and judging other people, look inward to examine and understand the root of your emotions.

The habit of looking inward rather than outward will lead to great spiritual progress. Emotional intelligence develops from the habit of self-awareness and introspection. Changing your outside circumstances may temporarily cover up painful emotions, but as long as you have not learned to witness, understand, embrace, and heal your painful emotions, painful emotions will return at the earliest opportunity.

Equanimity and Acceptance

Powerful emotions will not go away by anesthetizing them through addictive substances such as alcohol, cigarettes, or hard drugs. Nor will difficult emotions go away if you simply ignore them. Since emotions do not just disappear, eventually, you will be forced to deal with the negative emotion you are trying to avoid. The way to understand and resolve negative emotions is to feel emotions and witness them with equanimity, without being entangled.

Acceptance is the second key step for dealing with negative emotions. The longer you try to deny or block a particular emotion, the stronger that emotion will become. Acceptance is the opposite of denial or defensiveness; acceptance enables you to witness the emotion without resisting it or giving it power.

Authentic Emotions Are in Your Body

True emotion is felt in the body, not fabricated in the mind. Thinking and feeling are very different. Authentic feelings are always felt in the body, and not experienced in the intellectual mind. Thoughts always originate in the mind and can manufacture emotions. Emotions that originate from thoughts are mental inventions; these kinds of emotions are false emotions, not authentic emotions of the heart and Soul. Authentic emotions are messages from your Soul. Strong emotions felt in the body carry important messages that your Soul wants you to pay attention to.

Remember a point made earlier, every emotion produces a unique physical sensation in your body and induces changes in your breathing pattern. Emotions and corresponding physical sensations are always appearing and disappearing within your inner body. Emotional intelligence means maintaining awareness of these fluctuations and distinguishing your authentic emotions.

Emotions Are Messages From Your Soul

Your Soul does not speak in grammatical sentences; it speaks the language of symbols such as dreams, intuition, daily coincidences, etc. The Soul also speaks to you through your emotions. The person, who always knows what he is feeling, is in constant communion with his Soul.

Do not ignore your recurring emotions; they carry powerful messages from your Soul. Think of your emotions as wonderful friends who are trying to communicate what is best for you and what you need to learn during this lifetime.

Your Soul will not stop communicating with you just because you choose to ignore your Soul. Ignoring your powerful emotions is like sitting on top of a volcano — one day you will explode and burn with hidden rage.

The Two Basic Emotions

There are only two basic emotions in life — love and fear. All other emotions, both positive and negative, come from these two basic emotions.

Love is the sensation of the Soul (your highest Self). Fear is the sensation of the Ego. Whenever you experience love and love-based emotions in your body, you gain energy. Fear-based emotions scatter and reduce your energy along with your sense of wellbeing.

Your Most Painful Emotions

Your most painful emotions are those related to your old beliefs and hurts generated during the first seven years of life. These old hurts are now buried deep in your subconscious mind as *my life story*. People construct powerful defenses and resistance in order not to feel these old beliefs filled with hurt. Unfortunately, whatever you resist most in life continues to reappear in your life and cause you great pain. This process continues until you release your resistance and move on to grow spiritually.

How We React to Powerful Emotions

When encountering powerful emotions, we have all of the following experiences:

First, the emotion puts us into a trance. A trance is defined as "narrowing of consciousness". We see nothing but the powerful emotion. We slip into a trance when we unconsciously go back to our old traumas.

Second, we become thoroughly associated with the emotion. We become the emotion. We think we are the emotion. We forget that we are a vast Being and that a passing emotion is only a small cloud in an infinite sky (Being).

Third, we block out the event that triggered the powerful emotion. We try to dissipate emotional energy through various defense systems. It is so important to understand and acknowledge these defense systems that I will describe them in more detail below.

The fourth thing that happens when we encounter powerful emotions is that we hold emotions somewhere in our body tissue. Our physical tissue (including muscles) is a reservoir of undigested and unacceptable painful emotions.

Various Defense Systems

Our ego invents defense systems in the hope that we do not feel our inner pain. Here are some of the most typical defense systems that people create:

Anger

One way to not feel our emotions is to get angry and fly into a rage. When you express your rage at another person, you are actually manipulating that person in order to get what you want. You cannot feel your anger when you fly into rage. You can only feel your anger in your inner body through deep awareness of thoughts, emotions, and corresponding physical sensations while you are in that state. Again, this kind of awareness is emotional intelligence.

Pleasing Others

Another way we defend ourselves against feeling our own emotions is to place all our attention on the needs of others. When you focus intensely on what others are feeling or wanting, you forget what you are feeling yourself. Pleasing others or obsessive caretaking is another way of manipulating other people to get what you are afraid to ask for directly. Because you feel powerless in fulfilling your own primary needs, you please other people, hoping that others will fulfill your needs if you make them happy.

Hyperactivity

This is another way we escape our painful emotions. We stay so preoccupied with various projects that we do not have an instant to feel our authentic emotions. Through hyperactivity and work holism, we are too busy taking care of work emergencies instead of feeling our authentic emotions. This type of person goes from one project to another, non-stop. The particular projects are irrelevant, what is important to the workaholic is never stopping long enough to feel her inner pain.

Boredom

Some people, who are hurt deeply at one point in their lives, decide never to participate in life and never to feel life again — they make a subconscious decision to be bored with everything; some of them sleep until noon and are always yawning. The person, who is fully alive, acknowledges and respects all of life; the emotionally numb person is bored with all of life.

Daydreaming

Many people are emotionally afraid to live passionately and achieve their highest and most fulfilling dreams. They invent a defense system which is a life made up of senseless wandering and meaningless distractions. Of course, none of these distracting activities are gratifying to the person because none of these activities bring that person closer to the desires of his Soul.

Addictions and Drug Abuse

One of the fastest and easiest ways to numb our powerful emotions is to anesthetize ourselves with drugs or any other addictive activity such as over-eating, gambling, watching pornographic movies, and obsessive shopping. All addictions serve to numb our emotional pain. We become addicted in order not to feel our powerful negative emotions.

Sexual Addiction

Although this defense belongs to the category above, sexual addiction is so powerful and widespread that it needs its own separate heading. At the moment of this writing, it is estimated that two-thirds of the world's Internet traffic is sex related. Sexual addiction is a very powerful addiction; at the moment of unconscious sexual attraction, we lose much of our awareness and we fall into a sexual trance. The person we have sex with is unimportant; what is important is to block our inner pain through the powerful ecstasy of sexual orgasm. Sexual addictions are usually based on the unfulfilled emotion of intimacy. The loneliest people typically have very powerful sexual addictions. Sexual addiction also comes from repressed emotions of powerlessness and feeling unlovable and unworthy.

Psychosomatic Diseases

We create diseases such as depression, lethargy, migraine headaches, and chronic back aches, in order to not feel our gloomy sadness and hopelessness, insecurity, unworthiness, and distrust. As long as we are desperately ill there is no space for feeling our true emotions, because any disease and illness commands our full attention. We unconsciously invent disease in order not to feel the real cause of illness — our powerful underlying emotions.

Fully Experiencing Emotions By Letting Them Flow

The next time you are experiencing difficult emotions, relax your body and let powerful emotions totally envelope you. Fully embrace and accept powerful emotions by allowing them to flow through you. Do not resist anything; just maintain awareness of the emotion by maintaining contact with your breathing. Open up all your five senses and let the wave of emotional energy come in and flow through you while you witness.

The particular emotion is never the obstacle; it is holding on to or resisting the emotion that causes suffering. You must learn to be an open conduit for powerful emotions to flow through your body.

Emotional Intelligence – How to Fully Experience Our Emotions

Emotional intelligence is staying aware and awake to all our emotions, corresponding physical sensations, and thoughts. This is a lifelong meditation onto itself. All day, every day, maintain awareness of:

- Various emotions

- Corresponding physical sensations in the body. Notice the

location of the emotional sensations, the intensity, and the movement of these physical sensations.

- Thoughts that arouse various emotions

Pain associated with difficult emotions is inevitable, but suffering can be reduced through total awareness and feeling of our emotional experience.

Once entangled in thoughts and emotions, we cannot gain insight about the causes, symptoms, and dynamics of the recurring emotion. If we could "see through the emotion" once and completely feel the emotion, we would walk through the darkness and access great spiritual insight on the other side. Emotional intelligence means seeing through the trance of powerful emotions. When you shed the light of understanding and feeling on powerful emotions, they will release their grip on you.

The trick is never to avoid powerful emotions and fears. Approach them as a witness with full awareness; witness the emotion moving through you without fidgeting or avoidance of the full experience. Do not try repressing or holding on to emotions. You cannot confine the flowing emotional energy because emotions are not solid matter.

When we sit and witness difficult emotions as they unravel, without reacting or becoming defensive, we participate in their wave-like flow of emotional energy through our body.

During the witnessing process, we learn not to identify with the emotion, but just watch it without reaction while fully feeling the emotion.

Remember, as long as you repress your emotions, these repressed emotions will continue to unconsciously control your life.

Five Principles that Reduce Suffering

If we learn to understand, internalize and follow the five principles outlined below, we will regain our power over difficult emotions:

1-Total mindfulness

Total mindfulness refers to practicing awareness and mindfulness regarding triggering circumstances, thoughts, subsequent emotions and related physical sensations.

2- Equanimity

Practicing equanimity and developing the ability to witness internal dynamics (physical sensations and thoughts related to emotions), with a "hands off" approach.

3- Emotions are Impulses of Energy

Realize that we are a greater whole than just our passing emotions. All emotions are only passing impulses of energy. The real you is Consciousness witnessing passing emotions. Learn to "completely experience" emotions by participating in the wave-like activity of the emotion. When we collapse into our powerful Soul-Self, we experience all emotions as passing waves of energy. Experiencing emotions as waves teaches us that emotions are momentary and passing. We are not our emotions. We are the sky; emotions are just passing clouds.

4- Transforming Negative Emotions

Remember emotions are just energy and it is foolish to try to repress or hold on to something that is fluid or non-solid like a wave of emotional energy. You can, however, transform the energy of negative emotions by substituting the contrary positive emotion. Do this consciously. Whenever you do not like your emotions, just change the thought that created that negative emotion.

5- Different Vibrational Frequencies of Emotions

All emotions are made of the same Life Force (*Shakti*). However, each emotion vibrates at a different frequency. Love is the highest vibration and shame exhibits the lowest frequency. Strive toward embracing emotions with higher vibrational frequencies.

Ways We Express Our Emotions

There are four basic ways we express our emotions. Other variations are just combinations of these four basic habits:

1. **Internal expression** through mindfulness/equanimity. Emotional expression fully reflects your true inner state.

2. **External expression** such as acting out, screaming, facial expressions, crying, etc. This form of expression is just blowing off steam. It is not effective or transforming because the person is not in touch with the actual cause of his emotional outburst.

3. **Internal suppression** or numbing of authentic or severely controlling feelings. This habit is extremely destructive and leads to all kinds of addictions and illnesses. In the more severe cases suppression of authentic emotions leads to suicide.

4. **External suppression** or acting as if nothing is wrong. Have you ever known a person who always responds with "I am just fine", every time you ask him *how are you doing?* This is a common response for someone externally suppressing their emotions.

Of the four possibilities, internal expression with mindfulness and equanimity (number 1) is the healthiest because the person utilizes emotional intelligence to sense what exactly she is feeling before expressing that emotion to anyone else. External expression based on full internal insight is the next healthiest habit.

Freedom to Transform Negative Emotions

Positive emotions like love and trust vibrate at very high frequencies. Negative emotions like fear, guilt, or shame vibrate at very low frequencies.

We feel most joyous and energetic when we are vibrating at the higher frequencies with love-based emotions.

Emotions are just bursts of swirling energy. Instead of holding on or repressing, we can simply transform negative emotion to positive emotions.

Three ways to transform the vibrational energy of emotions:

1. Take a conscious action contrary to the negative emotion.

2. Practice creative visualization and imagine the exact opposite scenario that created the negativity in the first place.

3. Change your thought(s). It is usually a negative thought that creates a negative emotion. Whenever you do not like how you are feeling, just change your thought (the cause).

How Our Emotions Impact Others

Humans are broadcasting stations transmitting all our thoughts and emotions to the outer environment in the form of invisible energy waves.

The weaker, more scattered emotions quickly dissipate in the space within and outside you. These scattered emotions do not penetrate your environment.

Our most powerful, intense emotions are the ones that travel far into space. If you have a powerful, one-pointed emotion that you consistently feel, that is the emotion that travels far and affects everyone around you.

Our Strongest Emotions

Our strongest emotions are related to Soul-experiences and God. Our greatest pain occurs when we separate from our divine Source during the birth process. Separation from our divine parents is very painful and thus we tend to bury the pain deep inside.

Our greatest fear is feeling God within ourselves. Most people cannot tolerate the high vibrational frequencies associated with divine experiences. This may sound odd, but as a meditation master I can tell you that most people would do anything to run away from a direct experience of God within — without proper preparation, it is too overwhelming.

When your spiritual channels are opened, you are capable of experiencing the entire range of emotions, not just a limited spectrum. Take hold of your own power and know that your inner Guide already has all the answers.

Exercise in Developing Emotional Intelligence

Lie down on your back and begin relaxing by taking 15 deep Ujjayi breaths into your stomach. Take deep Ujjayi breaths into each part of your body. With each exhalation, release thoughts, tightness of muscles, and all emotional resistance.

Now, do a body scan from the top of your head down to your toes. At each physical location notice:

- Any corresponding thoughts

- Emotions underlying physical sensations and thoughts

- Physical sensations

After gaining insight on all three components, release all sensations, thoughts, and emotions with each exhalation and move on to the next body location.

Lesson 11

Money and Wealth

Money is just a reflection of our own creative energy. The actual piece of paper or coin does not contain any power or Life Force by itself.

We earn money through our creative energy (Life Force) and then trade that money, which is symbolic of our inner energy, with others for a different kind of energy such as our livelihood, support for our family, clothes, food, relaxation, etc. Thus, the entire economy of a country is simply the exchange and trade of vital energies between individuals.

The Secret to Abundance

The universal Life Force vibrating in all of us and in space is limitless. Therefore, the amount of money available to each of us is infinite. The more we are willing to open up to universal energy, and the more this energy flows through us, the more money we attract into our lives. This is the secret to abundance. Once we open up to our natural talents and tendencies and are in the flow of universal energy the Life Force opens up in us; money naturally flows toward us.

Those who allow the Life Force to flow through them understand that nature is full of abundance. Space never runs out of oxygen and the earth does not run out of dirt. So it goes with money and wealth; the amount of money and wealth are limitless. Think abundance all the time and wealth will chase after you.

We have to learn how to charm and call money toward us. Abundance mentality magnetizes you so that money flows toward you, but you must then take action in order to reel that money in. Right thought followed by action will most certainly make you rich.

Poverty Consciousness Blocks Abundance

The only energy that drives money away from you is the thought of lack or poverty.

Lack of money is merely a reflection of our blocking the flow of universal energy through us. Many people unconsciously block abundance and creativity. Even if nature opens up opportunities for them to gather wealth, their self-limiting beliefs about money deny these opportunities for wealth to materialize.

Many people living in poverty do not trust in the natural support that the God Force offers each person. Lack of trust in the natural flow of life is the root of our deepest insecurities. The whole secret of having money is doing what you want to be doing all of the time with unlimited trust that the Universe will take care of your needs. Poverty consciousness blocks this internal trust and notion of unlimited abundance from us, leaving us focused on and thus attracting poverty.

Abundance Lies in Following Your Heart and Trusting Your Intuition

To allow more of the universal energy to flow through us we must follow our heart, trust our intuition, and take risks to follow our intuition. As you follow this way of life fearlessly, more money will flow into your life. You must be willing to take risks toward opening the flow of universal energy in you. Wealthy people are usually very brave risk takers. Practice following your intuition in everyday matters while also fostering and nourishing your natural talents.

Money is actually God's reward for following our bliss. Many people follow meaningless careers; they are always struggling and just *doing* without a clear notion of their inner resources and God given talents. The spiritual truth that the Universe will actually pay you for who you are and what you love to do is hard for the mistrusting ego to believe, but the most successful and happiest people will attest that this is true. Those who have experienced abundance know the importance of following their heart and listening to their intuition.

The High Price of Attributing Power to Money

Many people think that money itself has a life, that money itself is important. These people take on work just for money, and although they can sometimes make good money doing unsatisfying work, they pay a high price in terms of health and stress.

This kind of livelihood where you think money has a life of itself always creates fear and struggle in your life. When you have a lot of money, you are fearful that you will lose it. If you have too little money, you are fearful and struggling to make ends meet. A livelihood that violates our natural being also makes us fearful. Activities that drain our Life Force essentially kill a part of us day by day, and therefore, we come to fear such means of livelihood.

Inner security can never be based on money. If you seek inner security based on money, you will always be afraid. All spiritual traditions teach that the ultimate source of security is within; we find inner joy and security by contacting our truest emotions and our Soul.

Many of us have been taught that life must be a struggle with very hard work, stress, and fear. As long as we insist on that attitude, we will refuse the natural grace of the Universe in rewarding us for our natural Self (*Being*). Increasing your vibrational frequencies through daily meditation puts you in harmony with the God Force making that much more abundance available to you.

We Are Caretakers for Universal Wealth

Another important point to realize is that our money is not really ours. We are caretakers for this wealth until it is ready to flow elsewhere. Since money is a symbol for energy, and all energy flows, money is meant to flow from one hand to another. Hoarding and stinginess constricts our Life Force and ultimately limits our potential for wealth. The less attached we are to money, the more money we will attract.

Visualize Unlimited Abundance

Because money is energy, it always flows in the direction that you need or envision. What I mean is that your consciousness, your deepest beliefs and desires, determine the direction in which money flows. You need to create a place, some space, for that money to flow. When you desire wealth, open up and create space in some aspect of your life for that money to flow into.

Remember, your consciousness stirs the subatomic Creative Energy; you co-create with God through your consciousness, subtle thoughts, and beliefs. If you always visualize having just enough to survive, that's where the money will go. If you visualize unlimited abundance, you will be open for nature's abundance.

Faith in God's Natural Support

If you are truly willing to do whatever the Universe wants you to do, you will always be taken care of, even when you get down to your last coin. Combine this way of life with a strong belief in unlimited abundance. Test out this spiritual truth — follow your natural desires with trust and faith; you will see that when you are down to your last coin, a door will open and more money will flow in. Keep witnessing this phenomenon until your faith in God's natural support deepens.

The stronger your trust of the Universe and your belief in abundance, the vaster your fortune will be.

Some Guidelines and Principles About Gathering Wealth

Once we have an understanding of the unlimited abundance of the Universe and the natural flow of money, we can start to observe our own relationship with money and make adjustments to ensure we are in the flow of abundance and wealth. Below are some guidelines and principles to help you attract more monetary wealth:

- I have already mentioned the first principle, which is that money has no Life Force in and of itself; it is you, your energy and Life Force that generates money. This is an important point to grasp; understanding this principle will increase your self-confidence because you will know that it is your inner resources that are income producing. Stop giving your inner Life Force and confidence away to the thought that money has its own external existence and power over you.

- Every person who has ever created wealth has begun with an idea. Every material creation, including wealth, begins with an idea. The source of all creation is the human mind. The key idea is that there is enough money in this world to make all of us rich. Once you focus your mind and convince your mind about a money making idea, your idea will stir all the surrounding energies and create circumstances that open doors of opportunity.

Thus, when you come up with a creative idea for making money, foster and nourish that idea. Never give up. All creative ideas and hunches that arise from within you are God-given ideas.

• The strength of your desire to manifest a financial goal is very important. All ideas and thoughts must be *emotionalized* in order to penetrate the environment and activate the creative energies. Strong desire is a powerful emotion. Those who follow their financial goals relentlessly and passionately leave no ground for retreat. Do not accept defeat at any cost.

• Avoid discussing your deepest passions and most powerful desires with too many people. Your lifelong dreams and most powerful ideas and desires are part of your private relationship with God. Your creative ideas arise from *a subatomic field of all possibilities* where all of creation takes place. Einstein called this field, *The Unified Field*. This is a vast energy field undetected by the five human senses. Only the recipient of creativity can sense the creative and divine messages. Therefore you cannot confirm the validity of your creative ideas with another person. Keep these creative ideas and innate desires in your own heart. Spend time alone for silent contemplation. During solitary hours of contemplation, you can nourish your creative ideas and strengthen your willpower. Initially, you should not even discuss your creative money making ideas with your spouse or children. If you ask for too many opinions, other people may talk you out of your project by superimposing their limited and fearful views on you.

• In order to accumulate wealth, you must be willing to expend energy. There is no such thing as *something for nothing*. If you desire a certain amount of wealth, contemplate whether or not you are willing to expend the appropriate amount of energy in order to achieve your financial goals.

- If you desire wealth, it is imperative that you are open and willing to receive it. Abundance is a form of energy, like everything else. If you block the energy of abundance, it will not flow in. Many people wish for wealth, but deep inside, they do not believe that they have the ability or worthiness to live in wealth and comfort. Examine your sense of self-love and self-worth. Can you accept wealth and comfort? Do you really believe you can be wealthy? If you are not open to the possibility, you will either lose money that you have accumulated or you will never become wealthy in the first place.

- The next important factor is having faith in your money making idea and faith in your ability to carry out that plan. Faith is a very powerful emotion. As I mentioned earlier, you must *emotionalize* an idea before that idea can mobilize outside creative forces to manifest your idea.

- Faith and love are the two most powerful human emotions because they vibrate at very high frequencies. The laws of physics teach us that any energy field that vibrates highly is powerful and can influence other energy fields at long range.

- Highly successful people maintain deep faith in their money making ideas. If you have no faith in your own idea, how do you expect another person to have faith in your project?

- Once you combine deep faith in your abilities and faith in your money making idea, you will send a clear message to your subconscious mind to organize your energy and arrange for the practical means for achieving your goal. Your subconscious mind also has the power to rally the support of natural forces.

- The next principle is that the fulfillment of your desire should bring you sincere joy and authentic wellbeing. What I mean is that a poet who dreams of publishing his poems will not be fulfilled with a goal of building a furniture factory. Understand your authentic emotions and deepest wishes; these are what you should link your financial goals to.

- Once you understand which area or profession you are interested in and most talented in, you need to educate yourself and become a specialist in that profession. General knowledge is good to have, but it will not generate a financial fortune. You must gain deep, specialized knowledge in your chosen field. If you feel you do not have the time or resources for specialized education, look for expert consultants who can advise you.

- Gather a group of advisors with expert knowledge about your field of activity. Make sure your advisors can work harmoniously with one another as a team. If you discover that certain members of your team lack faith in your money making idea, replace these individuals with other advisors who are self-confident and strongly committed to your idea.

- To reach your financial goal, you must have a strategy and detailed plans. Visualize every step of your financial adventure and translate these steps into detailed plans. Highly successful leaders do not easily change their plans once they have formulated the main strategy. If you find that after numerous attempts you have not succeeded, do not doubt your original idea. Rather, examine your strategy and plans, and make minor modifications if you must.

- Humans have three kinds of minds: the higher mind where creativity comes from; the lower mind which is the rational, intellectual mind; and the subconscious mind that controls vast amounts of creativity, energy, and resources. In order to succeed in any endeavor, you must send daily messages to your subconscious mind regarding your powerful desire to manifest your financial goal.

- In the field of psychology, this technique of sending mental messages to the subconscious is called *auto-suggestion*. Once your subconscious mind is convinced and believes in your idea, it will bring about the practical means for manifesting your financial desire. In the next section, I will outline the format of the message that you can send to your subconscious mind.

Daily Exercise in Auto-Suggestion

Twice a day, for about 10 minutes, send a wealth producing message to your subconscious mind. The message you send to your subconscious mind should contain the following elements:

- The exact amount of money you wish to have

- The time frame by which you want this money

- What activity do you want to engage in to earn this amount of money

- How much energy you are willing to expend to earn this amount of money

- How your money making idea will benefit others

In order for your subconscious mind to receive your auto-suggestion, you must relax your body and intellectual mind completely.

Lie on your back and breathe deeply into your stomach. Let each exhalation totally empty your intellectual mind of all thoughts. Take 15 deep breaths into your stomach and completely relax your muscles; with each exhalation, empty your rational mind.

When you reach a very relaxed and quiet space, repeat your auto-suggestion message aloud so you can hear yourself. While you are repeating your statement, visualize achieving financial success. Your creative imagery should include every possible detail; actually see yourself in possession of that money. Employ all of your five senses in these visualizations. Smell the scenario, touch it, feel it, taste it, and see it.

Here is an example of an auto-suggestion statement:

By May 15ᵗʰ, I will make $20,000 rendering interior design services to Mrs. Jones who will love my taste and find much joy in her new home. I am willing to expend sixty hours per week for nine weeks to complete this interior design project.

Other Important Principles Governing Money

The guidelines and principles explored earlier set the foundation for attracting wealth into your life. Here are a few additional laws governing money which will help you charm and further solidify prosperity in your life:

- Understand the three emotions that lead to poverty. How is it that some very smart people have little money and others with half the skills are very rich? Those who have a bad relationship with money have one of the following emotions regarding money: They either fear losing or earning money, harbor guilt about having money, or have underlying anger about money. If you want to accumulate money and wealth, you do not want to entertain or unintentionally nurture these emotions.

- Self-love increases wealth. It is impossible to become rich if we have a low sense of self-worth. We must value the self before we can lead a prosperous life. Ask yourself if you feel worthy of having comfort and wealth.

- Value your work. Ask yourself if you value your work and profession. This is related to the first point above. If you doubt or undervalue your professional services, your clients or employer will never pay you what you are worth.

- Remember, people first, money second, material objects third. Love of the self and other humans is the most important principle of life. That always takes precedence over money and objects that you buy with money. Also, your respect for money and a good relationship with money should precede your desire for material objects.

- Develop a respect for money. People who have no respect for money are always losing money. Money only comes to those who respect money. Do you have respect for the money you have earned? I have met people who do not even have checking or savings accounts; as educated adults, they still keep money in drawers or stashed away under mattresses! Others literally burn away their savings and wealth. Some people crumple bills in their back pockets. Many people are careless and occasionally misplace or lose their money. Money will respect you if you develop respect for money.

- Be careful what words you choose regarding money and wealth. Your words carry a lot of power. Your thoughts and beliefs give rise to words and words then influence your actions. Think rich no matter how much money you have now. Rich thoughts give rise to prosperous words. Examine your own words when you are speaking about money and wealth. If your words carry connotations of doubt, poverty, and eventual loss of wealth, your consequent actions will lead to poverty or loss of wealth. Do not engage in any conversations about poverty or lack. Do not complain about lack of money; instead, express high gratitude about all the abundance in your current life.

- Focus on long-term accumulation rather than instant gratification. Building wealth and prosperity requires work and planning. If you spend money based on instant desires and gratification, you cannot build up wealth. Work on internal happiness; the more contented you are within, the less you are tempted to fill your inner emptiness by throwing money into instant gratification. Make it a rule to save 10 percent of your monthly income. The minute you open a savings account, money will begin to flow into it—just open up that space for money to flow in. When your savings grow, invest them wisely, and finally, re-invest any income that you earn from prior investments; do not touch your investment earnings for a while.

Lesson 12

The *Guru*-Seeker Relationship

Every human being seeks inner harmony and peace because that is what we so often lack. Many individuals are unhappy because they lack wisdom. Sometimes we are at peace, but even then, we are troubled by our past pain or anxious about what may occur in the future.

The First Meeting With the Master (*Guru*)

When a student reaches a point where she is sincerely seeking inner peace, a Guide will appear. A Guide, or *Guru* in Sanskrit, is literally someone who takes the student from darkness into light. A student will recognize his or her Guide when the two first meet. There will be a magnetic attraction, an internal sense that *I can learn a lot from this person and become greater in his presence.*

The initial meeting between *Guru* and seeker is quite significant. The first meeting between a student and Guide is often an emotional experience for the student as the energy and message of the *Guru* resonates deeply within the seeker. A sincere *Guru* awakens the seeker's body, mind, and spirit. Upon finding their Guide a student's heart opens. The student is touched and deeply transformed by this union.

An experienced Guide quickly recognizes students who are ripe to receive knowledge. Such a student has reached a level of inner honesty and made peace within. The mature student has fewer inner conflicts and a more humble ego.

A students' level of openness and receptivity is an important factor because the God Force is very subtle and fragile energy. If the seeker resists the Guru or *Prana*, the Life Force will not flow through her.

The *Guru* and Seeker Relationship

At the onset of their association, the Guide and student take a vow to accept each other in this special association. The seeker stays in close contact and witnesses the Guru in many practical situations. Much of the learning and apprenticeship takes place during everyday circumstances.

The apprentice commits himself to the spiritual practices and knowledge being taught. This is a strict practice for purifying and strengthening body, mind, and spirit. The spiritual apprenticeship demands and induces certain changes in lifestyle.

Ultimately, all spiritual practices are about deep self-love. What the student learns through their apprenticeship with the Guide is self-care. The *Guru* keeps a watchful eye over each seeker and makes sure the seeker is truly grasping the concepts and practices. Of course, each student is responsible for their own discipline and continued practice. Remember, no one but yourself can calm your own mind and tame your sense of egoism.

Faith During Difficult Moments

In the beginning, the apprentice may have no direct experience of bliss or transcending the body, intellectual mind, or five senses. However, based on her trust of the *Guru* and the knowledge being taught, the apprentice vows to continue her study and practice even in the absence of awesome spiritual experiences.

Spiritual apprenticeship can be trying, long, and difficult. A wise *Guru* continues to stimulate, encourage, supervise, and coax the student throughout his journey.

Most students experience trying moments during their spiritual journey. These are days or even months when the student feels their meditation is shallow, their prayer feels false, or they think the entire spiritual venture is a waste of time. At these junctions, the student's faith in herself and the Guide weakens. Many questions arise during these moments of doubt. A student can feel as if the world is closing in on her when experiencing doubts about her spiritual practice, something so sacred and central to her existence. It is important to remember that periods of shallowness or doubt are merely a part of the process of spiritual growth. On the other side of doubt awaits faith and lasting joy.

An experienced Guide knows what his students are going through but purposely keeps his silence and quietly watches over his student. The Guide understands that moments of doubt and inner turmoil test and strengthen the apprentice's faith.

When there is no doubt, there are no questions. Seekers are often amazed to find a deep sense of inner calm in the presence of a realized master. When their faith is strong and they are tuned into the energy of a realized master, a student's questions disappear and instant answers burst forth.

Qualities of the True *Guru*

A true *Guru* is not interested in power, fame, or money. She is only interested in the sincere students, not in gathering crowds.

The enlightened Ones are here to show us the truth—how to live happily.

The true *Guru* is filled with love of the Soul. This unconditional love is an offering to any student who can receive this gift.

A true Guide of this world lives the principles that they teach. Such *Gurus*, like the Buddha himself, will not discuss any subjects that do not lead students to deep insight and liberation. This level of commitment is quite rare amongst Guides; there are a few precious ones that *walk their talk*.

Guides blessed with deep wisdom only teach what they have directly experienced. A Guide can only take students as far as s/he has traveled. Understand this concept—a Guide can only take you as far as his own level of realization, and no further. An analogy would be if you were to hire a guide to take you to the top of a mountain peak. Your guide can only lead you confidently through familiar territory; beyond that it becomes a situation of the blind leading the blind.

The most powerful *Gurus* emanate *Shakti* (energy of the Life Force). When you meet with a *Guru*, do not be concerned with the *Guru's* appearance, personality, or style of teaching. Rather, pay attention to the energy they emanate during talks and group meditation sessions. A Guide may be speaking to you about gardening, and you may think that you are listening to a talk about gardening, but later you experience an overwhelming sense of love and joy. Loving *Gurus* are broadcasting stations for the Life Force (*Shakti*). It really does not matter what the Guide is speaking about; simply being in the presence of a *Guru* fills the seeker with energy, love, and joy. Soaking in the joyful presence of the Master is called *darshan* in the Sanskrit language.

A powerful *Guru* established in Being encourages seekers to question the truth— over and over again. *Gurus* established in the Self have no ego. They are not threatened by seekers' resistance, curiosity, or objections. Therefore, feel free to ask your *Guru* any questions you want. As your faith in God deepens, you will see that you have fewer questions and deeper peace and silence.

Direct Experience—Your Ultimate Guide

Never take someone else's truth as your own truth—go within and experience the truth yourself. The only way to gain deep insight is to look within and observe yourself. Observe your motives, desires, and thoughts with equanimity and watchfulness. Just watch without reacting—this is what we do during meditation.

Without practical application, spiritual knowledge is merely an intellectual burden. Through direct inner experience, we gain insight and learn our own truth. Take the knowledge of ancient spiritual texts and scriptures from your Guide and apply these to your own life. Use this process to determine your weaknesses and vulnerabilities. Our vulnerabilities are actually openings for spiritual progress and great insight. Repeated application and internalization of spiritual knowledge will enable great progress in your spiritual growth.

Doubt whatever is beyond your personal experience. However, once you experience deep insight, cast away any doubts that arise from the mind and ego. Remember, the mind's habit is to think, then, doubt its own thoughts.

Meditative practice softens your heart and increases your compassion while enabling you to maintain a sense of detachment and equanimity. Daily contact with your inner Being charges your batteries such that you have more energy to help others. Yet, since you are less entangled with ever changing thoughts and emotions, a depressed person will not depress you. After all, how can you help a sad person if you yourself become sad? Meditative practice will open your heart with compassion, yet enable you to not be entangled with the constant fluctuations that you witness in your daily life.

The Benefits of Spiritual Practice

Meditation and other spiritual practices make a Muslim a better Muslim, a doctor a better doctor, and an artist more skillful and creative. We must become better human beings before we can excel in any area of life. Here is another important truth: the best way to uplift and inspire others is to reach your highest level of potential and Self-realization.

As we practice and apply our spiritual knowledge, we become lighter and happier because we come into harmony with our surroundings and our Higher Self. Once you have direct experience of your own inner truth, this truth permeates all aspects of your life. For example, a wise and joyful person in touch with the Self spreads that energy wherever they go. They are never lonely and find themselves surrounded by loving people because others desire to be around such a nourishing person.

Lesson 13

Kundalini Shakti

The Source of True Happiness

All human beings are seeking happiness, yet so many are dissatisfied for not having found this happiness.

Most of us mistakenly look outside ourselves for inner peace and contentment when we really have to turn within to find inner peace and joy. The only lasting source of joy is contact with your Soul, your inner God. Your Being is the embodiment of bliss and happiness. The closer you get to your Self (Soul), the happier you become. When you learn to respect your Self, you will respect everyone else and all of nature.

When you make contact with your inner God (Soul) your spiritual progress accelerates. You realize you are not just flesh and bones but a powerful spiritual energy field that is One with the same universal energy circulating in all of nature.

What is *Kundalini?*

The spiritual electricity flowing through every human being is called *Prana* in the Sanskrit language. As mentioned before, the same Life Force is called *Chi* in Chinese, *Qi* in Japanese, and *The Holy Spirit* in Christian traditions. This same vibrant energy when it rises up the spinal column is called *Kundalini Shakti*. True spiritual progress begins when you awaken *Kundalini* through spiritual practices and with the help of an enlightened master.

Kundalini has an outer aspect that energizes your thoughts, words, and actions on the external level — at the level of the material world. The external aspect of *Kundalini* also energizes all of your senses and your mind. Every human being alive enjoys the active, external aspect of *Kundalini*. The same way that electricity energizes a light bulb, *Kundalini Shakti* makes it possible for you to think, taste, smell, hear, and touch. Without the outer aspect of *Kundalini*, your body would drop dead in an instant.

Internal Aspect of *Kundalini*

The internal aspect of *Kundalini* is a reservoir of spiritual electricity located 6 centimeters above the tailbone. This spiritual electricity lies dormant in the majority of people. Once the internal aspect of *Kundalini* is awakened you are able to tune into the universal flow of energy. You realize, through direct experience, that you have access to the same creative energy field that pervades the entire universe. The awakening of *Kundalini* sets off a chain reaction that is essentially a transformational process that constantly heals your body, mind, and spirit. The God Force is within your body; you simply do not have a direct experience of it until the inner aspect of *Kundalini Shakti* is awakened.

The Location and Path of *Kundalini*

As mentioned above, the *Kundalini* force is located near the base of the spine extending over an area 6 centimeters along the length of the spine. Translated as 'the coiled one', *Kundalini* resembles a snake wrapped around Herself three and one-half times.

There are seven energy centers (*chakras*) and 72,000 subatomic energy channels (*nadis*) that conduct the God Force within your body. The main path for *Kundalini*'s travel is the *Shushumna Nadi*, a submolecular channel that is located at the center of the spinal column. Before *Kundalini Shakti* can rise up this central channel, two other secondary channels on the left and right side of *Shushumna Nadi* have to be cleansed of all impurities.

Meditation in the traditions of Kriya and Kundalini Yoga accelerate the cleansing process.

How *Kundalini* Works

Kundalini works patiently to remove all the blockages within your body, bit by bit. These blockages or impurities prevent the flow of Prana (Life Force) through your seven *chakras* and through the 72,000 *nadis*.

When *Kundalini* awakens, she travels through the upper six *chakras*, piercing all the subtle impurities that block her way. When *Kundalini* pierces the crown *chakra* (fontanel), you will forever realize your godliness. This is the state of enlightenment where you are permanently established in your Self, even during intense activity. Also, when *Kundalini* persistently resides in the crown *chakra*, you will perceive the God Force in every element of the universe—you will be in love with the day. With *Kundalini* coursing through you, you will fall in love with the day.

When *Kundalini* Awakens

As mentioned earlier, *Kundalini* is the Life Force or God Force flowing through the central channel of your spinal column. Because the God Force is all knowing, *Kundalini* knows your past and your future. *Kundalini* knows your body's capacity and how fast She can work on your inner healing.

Often when *Kundalini* first awakens, we feel sleepy and heavy headed. Before *Kundalini* can give us more energy, She must penetrate all 72,000 *nadis* and purify them.

Since all of us have some impurities and blockages in our system, when *Kundalini* starts to work on us, we may experience painful or emotional episodes. Some people become very ill, some feel back aches, and others may feel nausea. Not to worry, *Kundalini* actually burns up impurities that cause disease. Illnesses and pain brought on by *Kundalini* awakening are a sign that your body is cleansing itself.

During meditation, you may experience *kriyas* which are involuntary physical movements beyond your conscious control. *Kundalini* knows how to work on your body from inside out, from a very subtle level. She is like an internal doctor fine tuning every molecule of your Being. When we experience *kriyas, Kundalini* is performing special yogic movements in order to heal our body and open our energy channels.

Some people whose *Kundalini* has awakened feel the spontaneous sound of their mantra during the waking state. Others hear divine music and still others create beautiful art.

Effects of *Kundalini* Awakening

Kundalini regulates our breathing. Once *Kundalini* awakens we become so inwardly calm that sometimes our breathing comes to a standstill without the feeling of suffocation.

When this force awakens, you begin to see the presence of God in everyone and everything around you. You will experience a love so profound and unconditional you may cry for days or weeks. After experiencing this kind of love you may realize you had never experienced true unconditional love before.

With *Kundalini* awakened, you will develop the ability to remain detached while performing your worldly responsibilities.

When *Kundalini* awakens, your material life prospers. As you develop the ability to manifest whatever you focus on your business projects will progress and many doors will open in your life.

How to Awaken Your *Kundalini*

In rare instances, a seeker of truth will undergo spontaneous awakening of *Kundalini* simply through the divine grace of the God Force. Out of every 100,000 seekers only one might enjoy such grace based on his holiness during past lives. Barring this rare exception, *Kundalini Shakti* can only be awakened in a seeker by a realized master whose *Kundalini* is permanently awakened.

A master whose *Kundalini* is permanently awakened can awaken *Kundalini* in the student's body using one of several different methods:

- Training in regular and proper practice of Yoga and meditation

- Intense devotion to God and prayer. Because a true *Guru* is a living example of devotion and dedication to *Shakti*, the apprentice who follows the path of the *Guru*, usually develops devotion to God and surrender of egoism to prayer and Higher Forces.

- *Shaktipat* or transfer of the God Force through touch, look, or voice of the realized *Guru*. Those who transmit *Shakti* have received *Shaktipat* from their own *Guru*. The entire body and subtle energy field of the *Guru* is buzzing with the God Force. Even personal belongings of the Master are vibrating with a high frequency Life Force. *Gurus* who give *Shaktipat* through touch will transfer the God Force through one of three places in a seeker's body. They will either touch the area between your eyebrows, in your heart region, or at your tailbone (the root *chakra*).

- *Shaktipat* or transfer of the God Force through a look. The *Guru* who transfers *Shakti* through the eyes must himself have an inward gaze. These *Gurus* are totally focused on their inner Self and the flow of their breath into their inner realm.

- *Shaktipat* or transfer of the God Force through a word or *mantra*. The *Guru* who transfers *Shakti* through a word or *mantra* must have repeated that word thousands of times. When a *Guru* repeats the word(s) she enlivens the word(s) with her own vibrational energy of consciousness. Only a live *mantra* enlivened by such holy vibrations can awaken your *Kundalini*.

Lesson 14

Ego

Ego is the sense of "I, me, or mine". When we are born we do not have an ego. As babies, we do not feel separated from God, nature, and other people. This earliest sense of Oneness is based on trusting the flow of life and trusting that there are higher forces taking care of us.

Some time between the ages of 1 and 2, our five senses fool us into thinking that we are separate bodies out to defend ourselves against the world. Our five senses are part of our physical body. Since they are established within the body, the senses detect everything not in the body as "separate from me".

The five senses cannot detect our subtle body which consists of five non-solid energy layers on the periphery of our body. In total, we have six energy layers: one visible layer that is the physical body itself and then five non-solid energy layers in the periphery of the physical body. These more subtle energy layers include the outermost layer which is the Soul. The six energy layers of the body are:

- Physical layer (flesh and bones)
- Subtle energies (vibrational, electrical, heat, and electromagnetic energy at the surface of the skin)
- Mental layer (thought bubbles)
- Emotional layer (emotions)
- Intuition (deep wisdom and *Sixth Sense*)

- Soul (same as the God Force)

Know that your Soul is the same One energy of consciousness that flows in everyone and everything else and in the universe. There is no such thing as "my Soul" versus "your Soul". There is only one Universal Soul which is the subatomic energy of consciousness. Your Soul is the same as God, but your Soul is orbiting closer to your own physical body.

Being anchored in the physical body, our five senses are only identified with the physical body. Our five senses are not aware of the subatomic energy of consciousness, *Shakti*, which is the Source of all creation. Usually at around a year and a half, a young child notices and ponders, *this is my foot; I am separate from my mother; what if she forgets to feed me today?* At that very instant we have our first experience of fear and anxiety.

The root of all fear is the illusion of separateness from the one creative energy, *Shakti*. This perception of separateness of our individual ego is an illusion because at the subatomic level, everything in this universe is made of the same energy - *Shakti* or Pure Consciousness. Even the different faces you see on the sidewalk are the same divine energy of consciousness masquerading with different masks. Similarly, the core of every rock on the mountain side is pulsating with the same Life Force at the subatomic level.

All of our adult defense-systems form themselves around this basic fear of separateness. Ego is one of the greatest sources of our suffering because ego is based on fear not love. On the contrary, when you are identified with your lighter energy layers and subtle body during meditation, you sense the Soul. When you touch your Soul, you always sense love. Love is the emotion of the Soul.

What Happens When We Are Identified With Ego?

Sense of Loneliness and Isolation

Ego sees itself as separate from all else. Therefore, ego is the biggest cause of our loneliness and isolation.

Lack of Faith

Ego, mind, and our five senses are the parts of us that doubt our mystical and divine experiences. This is because our ego, mind, and five senses are not refined enough to detect the subtle subatomic and wave-like energy of God vibrating within us and the entire universe.

Control and Defensiveness

Since ego is identified with the physical body and feels isolated from all else, ego has a need to be in control of life in order to defend its vulnerable self against the outer world. Because of its sense of isolation from the Oneness of the world, it is counterintuitive for ego to trust the flow of life. Of course, both control and defensiveness are forces that create misery for us because they block the flow of the Life Force (*Prana*) within us. To live fully, we must flow with life. To be free means letting all of life enter us without fear or defensiveness. When your heart develops the strength to accept everything and reject nothing, then you will have the heart of a true spiritual seeker.

Seriousness

Ego is threatened by the "outside world", and wants to take control and responsibility for all life events which means ego takes life very seriously. Ego personalizes every event and critically ponders our reactions to past events. You may have experienced ego's questions in the form of – *because I did this, that happened,* or, *if I had only*

done it another way, maybe there would have been a different result.
These are all murmurs of the ego wanting to personalize every life
event, wanting to take on God's job; wanting to take responsibility
for all happenings.

People with injured egos take life very seriously. The internal dialogue
of ego may sound like this: *Life is hard, never trust strangers, I will
never fall in love again,* or *there is not enough money to go around.*

Unfortunately, everything you think, say, and do flows outward
like waves and vibrates within your environment. In essence, we are
human broadcasting stations. The subatomic God Force mirrors
your ego's internal dialogue and returns similar waves back to you.

Self-Importance

Our sense of self-importance and intense personal pride is a
characteristic of ego. The isolated ego feels very vulnerable in such a
big threatening world, so ego pretends to be powerful and important
in order not to feel its own vulnerability.

Another way ego heightens its sense of self-importance is by belittling
others. A big ego will make you feel very important at the same time
that it makes others feel insignificant or unappreciated. Contrary to
egotistical types, have you ever noticed that most individuals who
have made valuable contributions to our world are very humble
giants who love all of life and all societies?

Self-Degradation and Self-Confidence

Because ego isolates itself from the Creator, it can swing from one
extreme to another quite rapidly and without warning which has
a destabilizing effect on an individual. Ego can go from feeling
all-important and invincible to feeling intense self-degradation to

such a degree that a person feels small, unimportant, and powerless. Essentially, the ego either feels like a king or it feels like a worm. This constant fluctuation in self-confidence and self-image is a typical characteristic of ego-centered individuals.

Responsiveness Based on Habitual Thought Patterns

We experience most of our pain because we react unconsciously to old, conditioned thought patterns. A mind conditioned by past experiences lives in the past not in the present moment. Living in the past and responding habitually, we are unable to react appropriately to the needs of the moment. Due to this mental conditioning we experience pain.

Overcoming Ego Based *Samskaras* Through Spiritual Practice

In *Sanskrit,* our old conditioned thought patterns are called s*amskaras.* The ego wants our *samskaras* to survive because ego's own survival depends on the continuance of old *samskaras.*

Whenever you react unconsciously to your old thought patterns know that your ego is reacting. Meditation and spiritual practice gradually eliminate s*amskaras* as meditation practices also makes egoism fade. As a result of spiritual practice, your ego will experience pain because, after all, *who wants to die?* Whenever your ego is experiencing difficulty, be happy; it means your spiritual practice is going well!

Ego Is the Seen and Not the Seer

Ego is very self-conscious because it is totally identified with our body and five senses. Ego is that part of us which is obsessed about our looks, our clothes, our makeup, and what impression we make on others. In this sense, ego is the one who is "seen" by everyone. When we imagine how we look through the eyes of others, we become insecure and self-conscious.

On the contrary, your Soul is totally at one with everything and everyone else, so there is nothing to be self-conscious about. Soul centered people have no desire to impress or please others because the Soulful person is at one with everyone and everything. An individual identified with their Soul understands we are all intrinsically connected – there *is* only One.

What to Do About Ego?

It is a mistake to think we have to kill our ego for the sake of spiritual progress. Ego and mind are part of our physical existence on earth; they are part of our personal Self. If we attempt to kill part of ourselves, that part will rebel and make life hellish for us. If you try to force your mind to be thoughtless, the mind responds by creating so many thoughts that you feel you are going mad! You can never kill that which is a part of you. Besides, we need our egos to manage our worldly duties. For example, a medical doctor requires a healthy, strong ego, to manage the affairs of his hospital ward. The challenge for each of us is tuning into our Soul to positively strengthen and nourish our ego.

Integrating Ego With Our Soul

Spiritually, our challenge is to integrate ego with our Soul. If you continue focusing on your inner silence, meditate deeply, and serve others with love, your individual ego will flourish under the light of your Soul.

During meditation, ego melts and we make contact with Being, our Soul. Through continued spiritual practice, ego becomes integrated with the Soul. During deep meditation and silent prayer, ego begins to receive and carry out daily instructions coming from the Soul. When this happens, ego and Soul are no longer enemies. Ego simply carries out instructions from your Higher Self (Soul).

Twice a day, go into silence, receive your Soul's insights and employ your ego to implement the Higher Self's wisdom in your life.

Lesson 15

The Mind

The mind is our most powerful instrument; the mind is great and can help us achieve everything. Without the mind, even our body and senses cannot function because the mind animates our body and five senses.

The human mind can either take us to enlightenment or be the source of defeat and great pain. If untamed and a slave to the cravings of our five senses, the mind can destroy our life by becoming attached and even addicted to negative tendencies.

When we quiet the restless mind through meditation, our mind becomes concentrated. The concentrated mind is naturally ecstatic. The ecstatic state of the mind is called *Pure Consciousness*. We can access Pure Consciousness in the rest between two thoughts or the pause between two breaths.

Brain Wave Patterns Reflect the State of Our Mind

Brain-wave activity is a reflection of thought activity and how busy your mind is. EEG machines attached to the brain show that the brain can vibrate at four different frequencies or activity levels. Each level outlined below reflects the overall busy-ness or quietude of the mind:

Beta Waves: Beta waves oscillate at approximately 14 to 16 cycles per second as measured by scientific instrumentation. These brain waves are related to the busy, waking state.

Alpha Waves: Alpha waves oscillate at approximately 7 cycles per second. Alpha waves are experienced during undisturbed concentration (12 seconds of non-thought, or focus on a single thought such as the object of meditation). This is a state of *restful alertness* whereby your mind is empty but you have a strong presence in the present moment.

Theta Waves: Theta waves oscillate at approximately 3.5 to 8 cycles per second. Theta waves occur after 2.4 minutes of continuous deep meditation during which the mind is either empty of thought or focused on a single object of meditation.

Delta Waves: Delta waves oscillate at an alarmingly low rate of 0.5 cycles per second. A yogi in *samadhi* (28.8 minutes of non-thought) is experiencing the Delta waves while in pure bliss. This might cause a brain surgeon to be alarmed thinking that the meditator is actually in a coma, but a Yogi in *samadhi* is actually in a blissful heaven.

Concentration Leads to Enlightenment

When we concentrate the mind, we can accomplish anything. Without concentration we cannot accomplish anything worthwhile. Once you train your mind to tune into the silence of Pure Consciousness, your mind will know everything because Pure Consciousness is the source of all universal knowledge. Pure Consciousness is that vast, silent field that awaits you beyond your thinking mind.

Only you can train and quiet your own mind; no one else can do it for you. Take very good care of your mind. Be very selective about what you put into your mind.

When your mind rests in the vacuum between two thoughts its vibrational frequency increases. A mind vibrating at very high frequencies is uplifted and detached from negative thoughts. Negativity may come, but it soon falls away as the glowing mind remains detached and disinterested in negative thoughts. The glowing mind naturally gravitates toward empowering thoughts and notions. This is why a golden mind can lead you to a golden life.

Controlling the Mind Through the Soul

The wise person controls the mind through the Soul (Pure Consciousness). A mind guided by the Soul (*Atman*) feeds the brain with energizing and uplifting thoughts and enables us enough discrimination to register only useful signals from the senses. A mind bathing under the light of the Soul filters out all extraneous and harmful information.

The Mind of an Enlightened One

Here is how guidance is passed down the hierarchy in an enlightened mind:

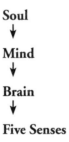

Soul
↓
Mind
↓
Brain
↓
Five Senses

The mind of an enlightened person long ago came under the influence of the Soul and its intuitive guidance. Because the Soul is made in the brilliant image of the God Force, a mind under its influence is totally mesmerized and in love with the brilliance of the Soul. Humans experience their Souls through the inward gaze; a mind in love with the Soul is naturally an inward mind, not one to be tempted by external distractions and desires.

For most people the above hierarchy or order is reversed. In the case of an ordinary person, the brain and mind are under the influence of the five senses and their cravings. The five senses get attached, are obsessed, and are even addicted to various external objects. The senses then pass on their obsessive desire to the lower mind (intellect) and agitate the intellectual/rational mind. The intellectual mind of an addict actually goes mad with incessant and addictive cravings.

This is how we build our own mental prisons; our compulsions, attractions, and addictions make the nervous system and mind restless and very tired. For example, have you ever noticed how you feel after six hours of window shopping at a busy shopping mall?

The result of continually obsessing about external desires is that we gradually lose our inner peace. This loss of inner peace occurs when the lower aspect of the mind (rational or intellectual mind) actually becomes enslaved to desire for external objects.

The Nature of Soul, Mind, and the Five Senses

Enlightened sages have further simplified the concept of the hierarchy of the Soul, mind, five senses, and the brain. They have broken it down for us to better understand and distinguish between the multiple layers of the human psyche. Below are definitions for the nature of the Soul, upper mind, subconscious mind, lower mind, the five senses, and the brain.

Soul

India's ancient Vedas say the human being is made of six energy sheaths, each vibrating at different frequencies. The Soul is the sixth and outermost sheath, the one that is least solid and most energetic. The energy field of the Soul vibrates at above one million cycles per second. The Soul or *Atman* is made of the same divine substance as the God Force.

The nature of the Soul is to know instantaneously without any doubt or analysis. The knowingness of the Soul is not related to linear logic or ration. All instantaneous and grand insights come from the Soul.

Upper Mind

The upper mind (*Buddhi*) is an electromagnetic energy field containing information. It is the link between the God Force and our individual personality. The upper mind is a vibrational energy layer that lies between our Soul and our physical body. The upper mind is the source of all insight, intuition, imagination, telepathy, telekinesis (moving objects with mind-power), and clairvoyance.

Subconscious Mind

The subconscious mind is another energy field outside our skull. Our subconscious is a storehouse of all our past emotions and experiences. This mind controls our most primal and powerful early-life emotions. Many of our emotions and habitual thought patterns find their root in the subconscious mind.

The subconscious is also where our core beliefs are stored. Since our beliefs ultimately control our behavior, psychologists claim that the subconscious mind controls 70 percent of our daily behavior. Unfortunately, much of human behavior is unwanted or conditioned behavior. In the yogic Sanskrit language they label such conditioned and unconscious behavior as *samskaras*.

Lower Mind (Intellect or Manas)

The intellectual mind is also a non-solid energy field that lies outside the physical body. The nature of the intellectual mind or *manas* is to think, then doubt and analyze what it just thought.

Another nature of the lower mind (intellect) is to constantly hop from one thought to another; the intellectual mind is obsessed with its own thoughts. Addicted to its own thoughts, it is impossible for the intellect to grasp the field of nothingness or Pure Consciousness accessible in the space between two thoughts. This realization is beyond its reach because the intellectual mind is composed of thoughts; therefore it has no direct experience of thoughtlessness.

Five Senses

The nature of the five human senses is to be fascinated with and enmeshed with external objects. Our five senses instantly form attachments or aversions to external objects. Both attachment and aversion cause us pain. The way to liberation is to witness all of life's sensuous temptations without attachment or avoidance. The concentrated and inward mind in love with the Soul can accomplish this.

The Brain

The brain is only a vibratory center that registers input from the senses and receives thought-waves from the lower intellectual mind fields that lie outside of the skull. Thus, your thoughts are energy waves that first arise out of the silent emptiness of Pure Consciousness. Thoughts then flow into your lower mind to be categorized and analyzed. Only later are thought-bubbles sent to vibrate in the brain. Since the brain is only a vibrational center it has no independent capability to think.

Characteristics of the Upper Mind (Mind-Field)

We were briefly introduced to the nature of the upper mind (*Buddhi*) in the passage above. Since few of us really understand the complex nature of the upper mind, our connection to the Universal Mind, it is beneficial to dive further into the explanation of this mind. Below are some additional qualities of the upper mind:

- The upper mind is one universal field of energy containing all the cosmic information we need.

- The upper mind has no fixed location in our body. Being energy, the upper mind floats as an energy field and is "non-local".

- The upper mind is not restricted by time or space. *Buddhi* can simultaneously access information about past, present, and future. *Buddhi* can see into far distant lands in a flash.

- The upper mind (*Buddhi*) is subatomic and therefore, undetectable by scientific instruments. This mind-field's vibrations are too high to be detected by scientific instruments and our five human senses.

- The energy of the upper mind moves faster than the speed of light. In other words, this is the fastest energy in existence.

- Our brain must be vibrating at the Alpha wave level in order to access the upper mind. Remember, the Alpha state is a restful state when brain vibrations are so low, that rambling thoughts no longer interfere with us contacting the higher mind.

- While our brain dies with the death of our body, the upper mind does not die when the body dies. The upper mind simply leaves your body and takes your memories to the next body that it adopts. This is how and why you have *déjà vu* experiences.

Actual Experiences of *Buddhi*

People who die, or are brain dead for a few minutes, and are later resuscitated, recall having memories of their life while hovering over their dead body. This proves that the upper-mind-field does not die with the brain; also, that the upper mind has an imprint of all our life experiences.

All memory is stored in the energy field of the upper mind and not the brain. Evidence that memory is stored in the mind-field (not the brain) occurs during surgery. Often enough, patients under deep anesthesia when the brain shows no activity will later have full memory of what the surgeons were saying and doing in the operating room. Individuals who are in a coma for months will have a clear awareness of people visiting and events occurring around them all while they were in a deep coma.

When creative ideas seem to come to you "out of nowhere" you are benefiting from your upper mind. Insight, intuition, and imagination are all activities of the upper mind not the brain. Remember, the upper-mind is the quantum field of infinite creativity and possibilities.

Being an energy field like the unified field of consciousness, the upper mind is one Universal Mind connecting all Beings. We can all draw information from the same Universal Mind. This fact is illustrated by the number of times throughout history that several inventors have created the same invention without knowing about the other inventors. The explanation here is that during that time period of history, the information about that particular invention was available in space and accessible to the 'one Universal Mind'. Each inventor just happened to tap into and implement the information received from the one Universal Mind.

Another example of one Universal Mind accessible to all is when two sisters report seeing their dying dad's image in the sunset at the same moment. Albeit different geographical locations, each sister sees the same exact image and message at the same time.

The upper mind, being a quantum energy field, is non-local and can instantaneously reach anywhere without brain activity. This is why you may have thought of a dear one and the phone instantaneously rang with that person on the phone line from two continents away.

Telepathy or the ability to transfer thought from one person to another, is yet another example of the non-local nature of the upper mind.

The upper-mind-field is not restricted by time. Whenever you have experiences of déjà vu or clairvoyance (seeing into the future) you are crossing a time barrier using your upper mind. As mentioned before, déjà vu experiences are also indicative that your mind-field used to accompany a different body in a different life.

Resonance—Are you Tuned In To God?

People often question, *if these divine vibrations are for real—if God exists, how come I don't feel or see God?*

My answer is, "If a cable-TV station exists but your Television set is not tuned into that channel, does it mean the cable-TV channel does not exist?"

As you have probably surmised from this rhetorical question, the reason most people cannot feel or see God is that they are not tuned into the *God Force* vibrating at very subtle, high frequencies. This concept can be further explained by using the analogy of how a radio and a tuning fork operate.

The way a radio set works is that there is an internal coiled wire in the radio set. When you turn the tuner button, you sensitize the coil to pick up only a specific frequency. That is how you tune a radio set to pick the vibrational waves of a particular radio station.

Another example of how resonance works is the functionality of a tuning fork. When you strike a tuning fork it vibrates at a particular pitch. Across the room, inside a piano, only strings resonating at the same pitch as the tuning fork will vibrate.

When we slip into the gap between two thoughts, or the rest between two breaths, we are tuning into the silence of Pure Consciousness. We connect with the Universal Mind in this silent gap between two thoughts. Within that void, you can access infinite possibilities.

Characteristics of the Subconscious Mind

Based on the brief introduction to the subconscious mind provided earlier in the lesson, you already understand that our subconscious is the storehouse of all our past emotions and experiences and significantly impacts our conditioned behavior. One of the primary goals of any spiritual seeker is to overcome their unconscious and habitual behavior, which necessitates understanding the subconscious mind. Below are a few more characteristics of the subconscious mind.

- The subconscious mind is also located outside of the physical body; it sits between the upper and lower minds and acts as an intermediary between the human intellect (lower mind) and *Buddhi* (upper mind). The subconscious has access to our intellectual thoughts as well as to the spiritual energy of the

God Force. This enables the subconscious mind to mobilize any resources you need to achieve your desired success.

- The subconscious mind acts as our internal thermostat. If you do not prepare your subconscious mind for a higher degree of success, the subconscious mind will only allow whatever level of success that it believes you deserve. When you convince your subconscious mind that you deserve, let's say a million Dollars or a wonderful marriage, it acts as a go-between you and the Soul to mobilize all necessary resources to manifest your desire.

- The subconscious acts very much like a radio transmitter. The subconscious mind converts your intellectual thought-waves vibrating at low energies, into ultra-high frequency waves, vibrating at or above one million cycles per second. Raising the vibration to such a high frequency enables the God Force to quickly hear your message. This is exactly what a radio station does; it converts the human voice into ultra-high frequencies that can travel through space. At the other end an ordinary radio set once again reduces the vibrational frequency of the voice message so that the human ear can hear it through the radio-set speaker.

- The subconscious records every incidence, thought and emotion in this and other lifetimes. It is a source of immense energy and intelligence. Once the subconscious believes and adopts a belief or life purpose, it contacts the spiritual energy of the God Force and manifests that thought or purpose using the most practical means available.

- The subconscious does not take time off. Your subconscious mind is forever taking commands from your intellectual mind. It pays equal attention to your positive and negative commands. So if you obsess about all the things that you dread in life, your subconscious will pick up those charged negative messages and solicit the God Force to bring about those undesirable outcomes. Remember one thing: negative and positive thoughts cannot simultaneously occupy your mind. So practice replacing negative thoughts with positive ones. When you feel negative thoughts, consciously release these thoughts with your outgoing breath.

Accessing and Programming Your Subconscious

You may wonder, *how do I contact my subconscious and program it with the right message?* The way to access the subconscious mind is to totally relax the intellect until mind chatter dissolves into nothingness.

There are four primary means of accessing and programming your subconscious, which will be described in more detail below. As you strive to access and program your subconscious, bear in mind that the most destructive negative emotions that strongly inhibit the power of your subconscious are jealousy, hatred, revenge, greed, superstition and anger. Avoid fostering these emotions; be mindful that if these emotions have taken root in your subconscious, they will be some of the more challenging emotions to overcome and reprogram.

Below are three methods for accessing and programming your subconscious:

1. *Autosuggestion*

As mentioned in Lesson 11 (Money and Wealth), autosuggestion is the practice of repeating a positive mental thought constructed in the present tense over and over again. If you persistently repeat a meaningful and powerful thought in your mind, that thought soon penetrates your subconscious mind and as soon as your subconscious accepts that thought, the same reality begins to manifest in your outer life.

You can plant any thought or purpose in your subconscious mind. The reason you want to construct these mental messages in the present tense is that the subconscious mind better absorbs messages in the *NOW* as opposed to messages having to do with the past or the future. The subconscious mind does not really care which thought or command you give it; it obeys each of your thoughts as commands. Of course, pictures work better than words. Therefore, try to plant your auto-suggestive message in the form of a mental picture or visualization instead of a verbal message.

Once your subconscious mind absorbs and accepts your message, your entire Being will be transformed. In fact, this is how hypnosis and self-hypnosis work. The hypnotist places the patient in a very relaxed state with an empty mind, and begins to make positive mental suggestions to the patient. The patient's relaxed and accepting mind begins to absorb and accept these suggestions subconsciously. Once the patient comes out of her hypnotic trance, the desired personal transformation will have taken place. I have helped dozens of student quit smoking by relaxing their mind and passing on anti-smoking suggestions to their subconscious mind.

Remember, once your subconscious accepts and believes your mental message, it enacts the help of the God Force to manifest your desires through whatever practical means available.

2. Love

In order to communicate with your subconscious mind, you must speak its language. Your subconscious understands emotions; you must emotionalize your thoughts. Therefore, any positive thought or purpose you send to your subconscious should carry powerful emotions. As you know from previous lessons, love is the most powerful emotion.

3. *Faith*

The second most powerful emotion you can attach to your thoughts is faith. Just like love, faith vibrates at a very high frequency; a frequency that the God Force is always tuned into. During deep prayer, you instill the powerful emotion of faith to your words of prayer.

If you pray with the faith that your prayer will not be answered (lack of faith), the God Force will obey and your prayer will not be answered. If you pray with total belief and faith, your prayers will be answered every time.

Important Characteristics of the Lower Mind (Intellect):

Based on the brief introduction to the lower mind provided earlier in the lesson, you are aware that the nature of the lower mind, also referred to as the intellectual mind or *manas*, is to think, then doubt and analyze what it just thought. Transcending the intellectual mind is essential to spiritual growth. Below are a few additional characteristics to help us further understand the lower mind:

- The lower mind takes the shape of any thoughts that you feed it. Although quite simple, this concept is really powerful. Imagine if you feed your intellectual mind with lust or anger, you will have a lustful or angry mind; if you think about God all the time, you will have a divine mind.

- The lower mind (intellect) is addicted to thought, therefore, it will hop from thought to thought. The lower mind will never stand still as it does not want to give up its addiction to thoughts. The lower mind hates living in the present moment. Do not try to fight the lower mind/intellect by trying to stop thoughts. You will not succeed! The trick to transcending thoughts is to witness and not identify with passing thoughts. The minute you witness the mind or wait for the next thought, your intellect will stop thinking!

- Wherever your lower mind goes, your five senses and *Shakti* (Life Force) go. The five senses are actually controlled by the lower mind; if you withdraw the lower mind from an object (called *Prajyahara* in Sanskrit), the five senses will quickly lose their craving for that object.

- The nature of the lower mind is to cling to the negative elements of life. So always aim the mind at high, uplifting places.

The Nature of Thoughts

In actuality, thoughts are the same as the lower mind since the intellect is wholly made of thoughts. When we think, we superimpose our personal reality on present-moment reality. So thoughts are our version of truth. The majority of people are deluded, walking around confined in their own heads, seeing the world through their personal version of truth.

Thoughts pull us out of the present moment. Thoughts block our momentary experience of life. Thoughts are always about the past or the future—never about the NOW. If you reside completely in the present moment, you will have no thoughts.

Most of your thoughts are other people's thoughts. As adults, we long ago lost touch with our own inner voice. Our thoughts are dictated to us by tabloids, newspapers, teachers, parents, TV and the Internet. Only by going inward, into the silence between two thoughts, can we hear our own *still voice inside*. This silent voice is the only truth relevant to you and your life.

The average person thinks about 60,000 thoughts per day. More than 90 percent of your thoughts repeat themselves from day to day. That is because you are unconsciously stuck in the same thought patterns and imprisoned by your core beliefs.

Thoughts are self-propagating. The more you feed or energize thoughts by thinking, the more thoughts multiply and amplify. The way to inner peace is to follow thoughts "upstream" to the Source of thoughts. Following thoughts "downstream" by trying to analyze them will only multiply your thoughts.

Thoughts vibrate and travel through space. Each thought vibrates with a different frequency. The more loving thoughts vibrate at higher frequencies. The more intense the emotion and intention behind a thought, the farther it travels through space.

The Source of thought, Pure Consciousness, is the silent gap between two thoughts. When we meditate on the gap between thoughts, the lower mind quiets down and we experience the present-moment reality of the God Force.

The Power to Change Thoughts

We experience life based on our thoughts, hence the old adage— *you are what you think.* No external circumstance can affect us; it is only our thoughts about a situation that affects us. Your thoughts determine your experience of life. If you truly understand this basic truth, your entire life will change.

Remember, thought-waves are impermanent impulses of energy; they are not solid, and they are forever changing. We have the freedom to change thoughts and replace them at will.

When we are identified with thought, we believe our thoughts are reality. One way to not identify with impermanent mental or emotional fluctuations is to witness or observe thoughts and emotions.

All of us also have the power to choose and change thoughts. When we find and develop the freedom to let go of negative thoughts and move on to more positive thoughts, we are exercising our ability to change thoughts. When we master the art of choosing and changing thoughts, we master the ability to manifest any reality since any physical reality is first envisioned through intentional thought.

Since our lower mind (intellect) can only experience one thought at a time, a destructive thought occupies just as much space as a good thought. Why take up precious mental space with negativity? We have the ability to immediately change our experience of life by changing our thoughts and replacing them with more positive and soul centered thoughts.

Talking is one of the primary ways we verbalize our thoughts. Too much talking agitates the nervous system, the intellectual mind, and because of all this restlessness, we lose our inner voice. One way to counter the negative effects of too much talking is to, once a week, practice half a day or a full day of silence. During several hours of silence, you will reconnect with your inner voice of guidance.

Understanding the 'Cycle of Illusion'

Most of us are caught in a vicious cycle that I call the "Cycle of Illusion". Here is how the cycle of illusion traps us:

EXAMPLE	DIAGRAM
Mother leaves her 4-yr. old and her abusive husband for another marriage	**Event occurs.** **And I attach a personal meaning to this event (my personal perception of the event).**
Child thinks that all women leave and are unfaithful to love "All women leave."	**I mentally recall the event, plus my perception of what happened.** **I then recite a repetitive recollection of what I think really happened.**
Based on thought repetition, this child grows up **believing** that all women are unfaithful.	**These repetitive thoughts create what become "My Core Beliefs"**
This child is now a grown up. He is now on his fifth marriage. He hires detectives to spy on on his wives, is abusive and eventually drives them away with	**My core Beliefs Influence My Behavior and Actions** **My Actions and Behavior Create My Life-Results (Self-Fulfilling Prophecy)**

controlling and jealous behavior.

Now, lonely after his latest divorce,
he shouts angrily,
"didn't I tell you, all women leave!?"

You can see from the above example that most of us are just living our lives collecting evidence to justify our personal beliefs about life. To break the Cycle of Illusion, it is important to realize that your personal perception (take) on what really happened is not utter reality. Most of the time, your core beliefs are those of a little child (like the above example), yet all of your adult behavior and your life results are being driven by the simple beliefs of a little child!

Stop it! You have the power to break the cycle of illusion!

Understand that your personal perceptions are not utter and solid reality. Release your self-limiting beliefs, especially if they are based on the naïve perceptions of a little child. Take the steering wheel of your life away from the inner child who is driving your life.

Lesson 16

The Human *Chakras*

The human body is much more multidimensional than it appears. What we perceive with our five senses to be our physical body is just a fraction of an immense energy system that is constantly pulsating and flowing within and around the periphery of our physical body. Surrounding our physical body and within our cells and tissues, an invisible subatomic Life Force creates the physical body and energizes all our thoughts, words and actions. The only reason we cannot see this subtle Life Force is because of its ultra-high vibrational frequencies.

Our five senses and this physical world constantly fool us into thinking that all of existence, including our own body, only includes those elements that scientists have so far verified with scientific instruments, and those things that we can perceive with our five senses. Once scientific instrumentation and sensors can pick up on ultra-high vibrational energies, even science will be able to verify the existence of the Life Force within every living creature.

As we continue our spiritual practice, our awareness becomes more refined. With this microscopic awareness, we begin to feel and experience the flow of subtle, invisible vibrations everywhere within ourselves and in the world around us. With this refined awareness, we experience a spiritual power that is the cause and sustainer of our physical body and the physical world. In the Sanskrit language they call the God Force pulsating in space, *Shakti*. The same subatomic energy circulating in the human body is called *Prana*. This same subatomic energy flowing up the spinal column during meditative practice is called *Kundalini Shakti.* The three names above essentially point to the one Creative Force.

The ancient Indian sages described centuries ago that all physical illness is based on imbalances in the Life Force surrounding the ailing physical organs. In other words, the health and balance of our Life Force (*Prana*) is much more important than later curing illness in the physical body that is actually the symptom of the pranic imbalance.

The human body possesses 72,000 energy channels (*nadis*) that conduct the Life Force (*Prana*) throughout our body. Amongst these conduits, 108 are primary. Seven of these 108 channels are major energy centers, called *chakras*. In the Sanskrit language, *chakra* means wheel; the Life Force spins clockwise like a wheel in each of the seven main energy centers. The Yogis discovered the *chakras* over 3000 years ago.

The *chakras* are connecting points between the human spirit (Life Force) and our mind and physical body. When these seven *chakras* are opened through yogic postures, *Pranayama* (controlled breathing), meditation, and the touch of a *Guru* (*Shaktipat*), you will experience a great deal of wellbeing and energy; your day-to-day perspective and experience of life will expand to the point of enlightenment.

Location and Function of the Seven *Chakras*

The location of the seven chakras are as follows:
1. Approximately in the area of the tailbone (*Muladhara Chakra*)
2. In the lower abdomen – in the vicinity of the urinary bladder (*Svadhishthana Chakra*)
3. In the area between the navel and the heart (*Manipura Chakra*)
4. The heart area (*Anahata Chakra*)
5. In the pit (hollow) of the throat (*Vishuddha Chakra*)
6. Between the eyebrows (*Ajna Chakra*)
7. Fontanel or crown of the head (*Sahasrara Chakra*)

First Chakra

The root *chakra (Muladhara Chakra)* lies at the base of the spine, near the tailbone, between the anus and the genitals. This is where human spiritual energy *(Kundalini energy)* lies dormant in most individuals. The dormant *Kundalini* is coiled around herself three and one-half times in the shape of a coiled snake. Once awakened, *Kundalini Shakti* moves upwards through the spine and pierces blockages and opens the flow of the Life Force through all seven *chakra*s.

The root *chakra* connects us to the physical earth, to our country, heritage, tribe, and family. All of our religious, cultural, and family related beliefs and allegiances are related to this first *chakra*. Energy in the first *chakra* determines how well we manage our life within the physical world. Our ability to stand up for ourselves in a tribe, family, or any other social setting comes from this *chakra*. When energy is flowing well in the root *chakra*, we feel very grounded, well connected to our family and home, and can easily manage our worldly affairs; we feel at home wherever we live. Those who have a weak root *chakra* are always moving, changing geographic locations; they never feel comfortable in any society.

The color or *halo* around this *chakra* is a bright red, like a tomato. Illnesses related to a weak root *chakra*:
- Prolonged lower back pain
- Sciatica
- Varicose Veins
- Tumors and cancer in the rectum
- Prolonged depression
- Any dysfunctions related to the immune system, such as HIV and AIDS

Second Chakra

The second *chakra* (*Svadhishthana Chakra*) lies in the lower belly (slightly above the genitals) and relates to our sexuality, money, one-to-one relationships, and creative abilities. The second *chakra* enables us to form sexual unions, create friendships, business partnerships and to develop personal power based on charisma, money and political clout. This *chakra* also energizes all of our creative activities such as creation of art or inventions. Energy to increase personal power as well as influence over others comes from the second *chakra*. People having a powerful second *chakra* can quickly take charge of any situation.

The color of the halo around this *chakra* is a bright orange just like orange juice.

Illnesses related to a weak second *chakra*:
- Prolonged pain in the lower back
- Sciatica
- All illnesses related to female reproductive organs
- Sexual impotency
- Problems with the urinary tract

Third Chakra

The third *chakra* (*Manipura Chakra*) is located near the navel. This *chakra* is where we hold the most basic beliefs about ourselves. This is the center of our self-esteem, self-worth and sense of honor. This *chakra* energizes our appearance, how we dress, what we think of our self; our physical and athletic abilities, and the perfection with which we accomplish our professional skills. If we find it difficult to receive a true compliment or if we have difficulty taking good care of our self (shelter, food, rest), we can be certain that we need to heal our third *chakra*. The more our ego integrates with our all-powerful Soul, the more healthy and potent our third *chakra* becomes. Integration of our ego with our Soul produces authentic power. A deep sense of authentic power arises as we heal our third *chakra*. To establish and strengthen your authentic power, meditate daily; let your ego bathe and release its defensiveness in the spiritual light of your Soul.

The color of *the halo* around this center is a bright yellow, like a lemon. Illnesses related to a weak third *chakra*:

- Arthritis
- Gastric ulcers
- Diseases related to the colon and intestines
- Diabetes and pancreatic dysfunctions
- Indigestion
- Bulimia and anorexia
- Diseases of the liver
- Hepatitis
- Adrenal disorders

Fourth Chakra

The fourth *chakra (Anahata Chakra)* is located at our heart-center, which in yogic terms, is found at the center of our chest cavity. This *chakra* is the source of all our emotions. The heart-center is the source of love and hatred, well wishing and resentment, anger and kindness—you can see that all polarities are part of the reality of life; they all co-exist. All emotions, negative and positive, are lodged in the heart *chakra*. This is a very powerful *chakra* because our heart commands so much of our emotional energy. Your heart can either make you bitter or fill you with joy and love. Emotions involving judgment, hatred, envy, jealousy and shame drain the Life Force out of this *chakra*. The biggest challenges in healing this *chakra* are to learn compassion, unconditional love and forgiveness.

The color of the *halo* around this energy center is a rich green, like a grassy meadow at springtime.

Illnesses related to a weak heart *chakra*:

- Heart failure
- Heat attacks
- Irregular heartbeat
- Asthma and all forms of allergies
- Lung cancer
- Bronchial pneumonia
- Cancer in the upper-back, shoulder, and breast

Fifth Chakra

The fifth *chakra* (*Vishuddha Chakra*) lies at the base of our throat. This *chakra* controls our willpower, the power of personal choice and our ability to speak out our personal truth. A powerful fifth *chakra* supports us in following our biggest dreams; with a healthy fifth *chakra*, we have an easier time making major decisions at critical junctions. When this *chakra* is weak, we develop various addictions and lose the willpower to quit addictions. From this *chakra*, we gain the strength to express our true voice and opinions to the world. With a strong fifth *chakra*, our unique and most sincere voice is heard!

The color of the *halo* around this energy center is light blue, like the sky.

Illnesses related to a weak fifth *chakra*:

- Scratchy throat
- Frequent sore throats
- Ulcers within the mouth
- Gum disease
- Problems in the joints
- Scoliosis
- Laryngitis
- Swollen glands
- Thyroid problems

Sixth Chakra

The sixth *chakra (Ajna Chakra)* is located between the eyebrows, a few inches inward toward the brain. This is the center of wisdom—*the Third Eye*. People with a healthy sixth *chakra* can step into any situation and quickly distinguish the apparent, superficial reality from the true, underlying reality.

This center also enables us to challenge and dispose of outdated beliefs that no longer serve us. The sixth *chakra* relates to the power of insight and intuition, to our power of seeing beyond the apparent reality. A healthy sixth *chakra* gives us the capacity to learn from life's experiences and not repeat the same mistake over and over again. The unhealthy aspect of this *chakra* creates arrogance and cynicism. A healthy sixth *chakra* makes us wise and intuitive.

The color of *Prana* circulating in this energy center is bluish-purple, what some people call cobalt blue.
Illnesses related to a weak sixth *chakra*:

- Brain tumors and strokes
- All neurological dysfunctions
- Blindness and deafness
- Diseases related to the spinal column
- Learning disabilities
- Seizures

Seventh Chakra

The seventh *chakra (Sahasrara Chakra)* is located at the top of our head and acts like a powerful magnet that pulls us upward toward the light of God. This *chakra* is the center of our spiritual hope and faith in the God Force. This center constantly whispers a message reminding us that our life is more than the gathering of material possessions. When this center begins to open up, we ponder questions like: *What or who is God? For what purpose was I born? Who created the Universe? How can I connect with the One Source who created all of this?* Once this *chakra* opens up, we experience blinding white light during or after meditation sessions.

Those who fail to develop this *chakra*, suffer from much fear, anxiety and depression because they remain routed in the two-dimensional, material reality which is not the Source of our life. Those who live solely based on gathering material possessions and rational, scientific logic inevitably dry up and sink into depression as their Spirit withers. Pay attention to those parts of you which you cannot express in logical terms—dreams, emotions, deep wishes, intuition, creative impulses, etc. These are ways that your Soul expresses itself to you.

With a healthy and open seventh *chakra*, we are able to trust the natural flow of life. We enjoy so much inner-bliss that we can give selflessly to others. Such people enjoy deep faith and devotion; they are involved in humanitarian efforts; they are a source of spiritual inspiration for others.

The color or halo around this energy center is a milky white.
Illnesses related to a weak seventh *chakra*:
- Energetic disorders
- Depression related to loss of contact with God
- Prolonged physical exhaustion
- Extreme sensitivities to light, sound, and other harsh elements in the outer environment

Lesson 17

Understanding and Managing Fear

There are basically two types of fear:

1. Fear of danger and physical harm

2. Psychological fear

The first type of fear is very useful because it can save your life; this type of fear is real because it is instinctual, not psychological.

The second type of fear, psychological fear and worry, is unreal; this type of fear is always an invention of our ego and mind. You cannot eliminate fear through techniques because psychological fear essentially does not exist as an objective reality. The only way to eliminate psychological fear is to understand and witness it. Once we understand what fear is, it loses its power over us. When we witness our own states of fear and worry while maintaining breath awareness, fear and worry dissolve.

If you comprehend the following statement, you will truly understand psychological fear:

Fear is the expectation of an undesirable event in the future.

If you understand and accept the above truth, you also understand that people, who truly live in the present moment, have no fear—

fear is always about a prediction about a future event. This is why fear of a future event is unreal, because very few people can truly predict the future. Also, fear of a future event is never as scary as facing that occasion at the moment that it actually arrives. There are millions of people who fear the thought of death, yet when the actual moment arrives, they are calm and ready to go because when the Soul leaves the body and people are liberated they experience absolute bliss and joy. Ask those who have died for a few minutes and have later been resuscitated. Fear of death is always more scary than the moment of death.

The Roots of Fear and Worry

The primary root of fear is our perception of separateness from Spirit or the God Force that we are made of. Fear enters our consciousness whenever we are identified with anything outside our inner Self (Soul). Identification with external forces takes our attention away from our inner Self, causing us to lose contact with our own essence, and experience fear. When we strongly identify with external phenomena such as our country, income-level, family, social status, and fame, fear creeps in.

Another source of fear and worry is not being present in this moment. When we are trapped with thoughts of the past or future, the mind begins to wander and when the mind wanders from the present moment, fear and worry creep in. To become more present, be aware of your breath coming in and going out, and also your bodily sensations. Through breath and body consciousness, we can live in the present moment which is devoid of fear and worry.

Fear Causes Us to Doubt Our Inner Wisdom

Fear causes us to doubt our inner wisdom and forces us to obey unjust external authorities. Whenever we fear an enemy, we give away our power to that enemy. There are dozens of societies today being ruled by evil and unjust laws. Leaders of these societies force their people into subjugation through fear.

Those who regularly maintain their spiritual practice, live by self law instead of national, cultural and tribal laws. Yet, in a moment of fear, we doubt our inner Self and relinquish our inner wisdom and intuition to an external authority. Spiritually speaking, that moment is the beginning of our misery and weakness.

It is important to recognize how fear operates in our lives. When we understand how fear controls us, we truly begin our spiritual journey.

Managing Our Fears

Once we begin to recognize how fear presents itself and impacts our lives, it is crucial to work on conquering the crippling power fear has on us. Below are some powerful suggestions for managing your fears:

Face Fears Directly

Whenever you try to avoid fear, you just perpetuate it. If you are scared of an up-coming event, stay in the present moment, then, when the occasion arrives, simply jump into the situation while maintaining awareness of your inhalation and exhalation. Here, I am not asking you to breathe; I am asking that you stay mindful of the motion of your inhalation and exhalation while you are facing your fears. Once you are face-to-face with that scary situation, you will be intensely present and will successfully manage the situation with present-moment awareness, spontaneity, and breath consciousness.

Just Take Care of this Moment

Regretting the past or worrying about the future is a pure waste of energy. There is nothing you can do about the past or the future; just take care of what you can in this moment. This moment is the only thing you have got to work with. If there are circumstances in this moment that are beyond your reach, fix what you can and leave the things you cannot fix to Higher Powers.

Do Not Try to Change the Situation; Change Your Mind

Ultimately, your fears and worries do not arise from the situation; rather, it is the way your mind perceives a future circumstance that creates fear and worry. When your mind becomes fearful and worried, continue to bring your focus back to your breathing and the present moment.

Become Aware of Your Breathing

Changing your breathing pattern will immediately affect your emotions and state of mind. Steady, slow, deep breathing into the stomach area will calm your mind and emotions. Breath awareness also brings you to the present moment where fear does not exist.

Visualize a More Positive Future Outcome

You are probably scared because you are imagining an undesirable future scenario. As we explored in previous lessons, creative visualization is a powerful tool for activating the subconscious mind; spend time visualizing a more positive future outcome and your fear will dissipate. Visualize an outcome that will be more comforting to your mind. For example, if you are flying in turbulent skies and you are visualizing that the wings of the aircraft are breaking off, become mindful of several slow, rhythmic, and deep breaths, then visualize that the airplane is riding safely on the huge, luminous palm of the God Force.

Take Immediate Action

Whenever you are scared of an upcoming situation, take a few breaths, step right in, roll up your sleeves and simply take action. You will see that taking action to resolve a future problem immediately reduces your level of fear.

Meditation

Meditation eliminates our identification with the intellectual mind and ego. During deep meditation we experience the Soul. Soul has no fear; it only experiences love and God in everything. Make time for meditation in your daily routine.

Other Facts to Understand About Fear

- Often, our lives wind up exactly where we feared it would. This is because when we are fearful we are concentrating on whatever it is that we fear. As mentioned in Lesson 5 (The Quantum God), modern quantum physics experiments show that our concentrated and focused thoughts influence the creative dance of the atom, and because everything is made of atoms, the fearful thoughts we broadcast outward are like magnets that manifest exactly the situations we fear most.

- The reason so many people concentrate on and obsess about fear is that fear is a painful energy we want to avoid. Because fear is so painful we concentrate intensely on avoiding it, not knowing that whatever we pay attention to grows! If we concentrate on fear itself, we will experience fear over and over again until this fear literally paralyzes us. So, the fear we are obsessing about becomes so magnified through sustained attention that it takes over our entire presence.

• Fear constricts us; we no longer feel expanded and liberated such as we do when we are in contact with our inner Self.

• Fear is the loss of something material as imagined by the ego; the loss of anything perceptible by the five human senses—money, fame, beauty, reputation, power, etc., creates fear.

• At the height of fear, the point of total paralysis, the petrified ego momentarily collapses and the universe gives us a momentary window of time to see through the illusion of fear. At the instance of the petrified and paralyzed ego collapsing we realize that we are Spirit—indestructible and eternal.

Defensiveness

Fear is painful to feel, and in order to avoid feeling it, we build a fortress of defenses to protect ourselves. Examples of common defense mechanisms are: addictions, work holism, rage, apathy and boredom toward life, daydreaming and being distracted, and pleasing others in order to not feel your own feelings.

Change and progress are the nature of life. We block change through fear induced defense mechanisms. Just like fear, defensiveness constricts our consciousness and our energy fields; our defenses block the flow of the Life Force (*Prana*).

Defenses are guards against past or future fears—they numb our awareness regarding the present moment, where God lives. For example, if someone broke your heart years ago, you might fear that love will again break your heart. So, you put a defense against a wonderful person approaching you in this moment.

By doing so, you lose the beauty of the moment and that beautiful person.

When we identify our defenses and realize they no longer serve us, we can release them and become free. Freedom brings power. The free person is a very powerful person.

Physiological Reactions to Fear

We have discussed the way our mind creates fear by identifying with external factors and negating the present moment. As the message of fear, originating in the mind, takes hold in our body, we experience physiological reactions. Below are some of the physical reactions that occur when we are fearful:

- Adrenaline, a fight-or-flight chemical that puts our mind and nervous system in extreme alert state, is pumped into the blood stream
- Racing heart
- Shallow, rapid breathing
- Veins and arteries sink lower beneath the skin
- Tightening of all muscles
- At an extreme level, the adrenals flood the body with steroids that can send us into shock

Psychological Reactions to Fear

In addition to identifying the physiological symptoms of fear it is imperative to recognize the psychological reactions that arise in response to fear. The challenge of identifying the root 'cause' of our fear, or what made our mind adapt a state of fear, requires sifting through the web of emotions and often debilitating states of mind that are linked to fear. Examples of psychological reactions to fear include:

- Confusion
- Mind chatter
- Anger
- Jealousy
- Envy
- Greed
- Violence

Lesson 18

Steps Along the Spiritual Journey

Your spiritual journey is the beginning of an intentional search for truth and connection with your inner God. This search may begin before or after the start of your formal spiritual practices such as prayer, meditation, and yogic postures (*Asanas)*.

When we first begin our journey we may feel frightened because we think we are all alone in our search for the inner God. While you may feel alone, you are definitely not alone. To provide you with assurance and support, I thought it a good idea to describe signs and symptoms that dozens of other students have experienced during their inner journey.

- The spiritual journey begins with a deep yearning for truth. Many spiritual seekers grow increasingly uncomfortable with the life routine they maintained during prior years. Instinctively at such a junction, we know that something about our life is changing and that we can never go back to our prior life routine again. I like to use the analogy of a foot that has outgrown its shoe; in the same way we may feel as though we have outgrown our previous life. At this point, we may feel depressed and lack energy and enthusiasm for our daily routine. At such a beginning, when we start our inner work, many of us feel isolated and estranged from old friends. Some of us even feel distanced from our spouse or lover.

- Usually we reach a point of pain and meaninglessness in our lives that triggers an intentional, persistent, and focused exploration of our inner world in order to make contact with a source of serenity and wisdom. It is as though you have a powerful desire to see that mystical dimension which lies beyond the visible world of the five human senses.

- Another sign that you have begun your spiritual journey is a sense of disillusionment and mistrust of the external order of things. When we realize that parts of our lives just aren't working, and that the external world and all of its authorities are themselves in a state of panic, fear and chaos, we no longer follow societal, cultural, and tribal laws. We have reached a point where we are no longer willing to surrender our internal power to external authorities. Instead, we live by self-rule; this means we refer to our inner Guide, rather than external authorities, for daily guidance. Our inner Voice becomes the only true voice that we trust.

- At this stage, many spiritual aspirants become disenchanted and bored with organized religion. The concept of an all-loving God who creates a heaven or hell no longer makes sense. Instead of following traditional religion and blind faith, spiritual seekers develop an insatiable curiosity and appetite for meditative practices and metaphysical knowledge. Any knowledge or practice that leads to Self-realization becomes very important at this stage. This is a stage where the aspirant can only make sense of direct contact with her own God, without the interference of any intermediaries.

- In the early stages of meditation, many students discover that they have spent a lifetime "living for others" instead of loving their own self. Whenever we base our life on pleasing others, we abuse ourselves emotionally and spiritually, and we also lose contact with our Life Force (*Prana*). Ironically, we never succeed in fully fulfilling the expectation of others and pleasing them.

- The first couple of times we dive into our own inner silence, we contact our most authentic essence. With this contact of the Self (Soul), we feel great love for ourselves and experience a level of self-confidence we have never experienced before. For the first time, we realize our true value and worth. Through deep inner work, we learn to develop personal boundaries for self-protection and self-care.

- Experiencing a new sense of love for their inner Self, students often question how this new found love for the Self differs from an ego-based love. Some students ask, *How do I know the difference?* It is important not to confuse love for the Self (your inner God) with the egoistic notion of narcissism. Self-love in the spiritual sense means worshiping the subatomic energy of God within you. Self-love means fulfilling your deepest emotional and spiritual needs. Self-love is any choice you make to honor, love and worship your own core. Narcissism, on the other hand, is based on a false self (ego) that is injured and needs to aggrandize and falsify itself. Your Soul is already a perfect reflection of the God Force; it has no need to impress anyone else. As your love for your Self deepens, trust that this new found love is pure and Soul centered.

- When our confidence grows, we become very interested in self-empowerment. We no longer feel vulnerable and powerless in a life that we thought was controlled by external forces. We come to realize that we shape much of our external reality through our thoughts and our mind. We literally see how our mind creates our reality. This is a holy stage because the aspirant clearly takes responsibility for every aspect of his life and forever casts away the feeling of being victimized by external forces.

- During the journey of self-discovery, we develop a taste for solitude and quiet time, a strong thirst for *Soul communion.* When we experience the fulfillment of spending time with our self, we come to understand the expression *sweet solitude.* This is the stage when the false self (ego) falls away and we hear our inner voice, our spiritual calling or mission. At this instant, we understand that our ultimate relationship is with our inner God. Even aspirants who have a very loving relationship with their spouse and children feel first and foremost in love with their inner God. Having realized that we are not really dependent on anyone to survive, we create new relationships based on mindfulness, honesty with ourselves and others, and mutual benefit. We no longer accept makeshift relationships based on the fear of loneliness and emotional desperation.

- Many spiritual aspirants develop the habit of interacting with nature—walks in the woods, hikes in the mountains, fishing by a lake, etc. Through their interaction with nature, many people develop a great rapport with the natural world and find regular communion with nature becomes part of their spiritual practice. A pristine environment within nature absorbs human negativities and recharges the nervous system with a renewed sense of calm, clarity, and optimism.

- Most spiritual aspirants are very excited by the self-love, self-confidence, and empowerment they feel at the on-start of their spiritual practice. Feeling empowerment and wellbeing, they may try to convince family members and friends to join them on this path. Unfortunately, more often than not, rather than exploring the knowledge and practice, others may think the aspirant has lost her emotional balance and may even ridicule the seeker. They may view your spiritual Guide and your practice with suspicion. In such cases, you should simply introduce them to the knowledge, then, leave the topic alone. Only speak to those who are genuinely interested and do not offer spiritual guidance or advice unless you are asked. Your inner silence and peaceful energy will be your most powerful spiritual statement—all you really have to do is walk through life with your serenity and love and other people will automatically be affected by your deep peace. We cannot depend on others to join us on our quest for self-knowledge. The fact is, while some people are ready for genuine inner work, the majority of people are simply happy with their familiar lives and fear any changes that a journey of self discovery might bring about.

• As your meditation and contact with the Soul deepens, you lose your need for external approval and may not even care if your loved ones approve of your spiritual practice. The still, inner voice becomes your faith and your inner God. This is not a stance of rudeness or apathy toward your loved ones; the connection with your heart and Soul is so strong that you love everyone while maintaining the highest level of allegiance to your Higher Self and inner voice.

• At some point during their spiritual journey, often during the beginning stages, students feel a need for a support group—a group of individuals who are traveling on the same path. A meditation center serves the function of bringing seekers and the *Guru* together on a regular basis. This kind of support is critical in deepening the seekers' knowledge and meditation practice.

- Progress along the spiritual path typically creates changes in our lives. Many people change professions, homes, diets and even the type of clothes they wear. Gradually our life becomes simpler; we tend to reduce our meaningless activities, focus more on our emotional and spiritual health, and prefer quiet time with loved ones rather than random and meaningless socializing. Material and professional goals become less important; we become more interested in "being" in touch with our inner awareness. However, throughout this transformation, the true spiritual warrior stays very active in the material world without being overly attached or obsessed with the results of activities. We simply play our role in a movie called "my life."

- Deeper meditation and awareness heighten our sensitivity to subtle vibrational energies of all kinds. Our five human senses become much sharper and many students begin to access multisensory powers of intuition, telepathy, and telekinesis (moving objects with mind power). As our inner radar becomes more sensitive, we react more strongly to negative vibrational energy coming from environmental toxins such as loud noise, exhaust fumes, unhealthy food, cigarettes, drugs, as well as certain kinds of apparel that irritate our skin. Picking up on subtler vibrations, many spiritual aspirants develop a deeper sense of compassion for the pain that others feel. Also through the newly enhanced senses, some meditators develop temporary allergies that later disappear.

- This heightened sensitivity to subtle vibrational energies usually brings about a temporary illness for the apprentice of meditation. Such illnesses are good based on two reasons: (1) illness calls your attention to your inner self; (2) illness caused by shifts in spiritual energy burns up all the impurities that prevent deeper meditation. When you burn up such impurities during spiritual practice, you are actually preventing much more serious illnesses in the future.

- Most students who are in the beginning and intermediate stages of their practice notice a shift in their perspective of life. It is literally as if we perceive the same life and people through a different set of eyes. One way to understand this concept is to imagine that you have changed the prescription of your eyeglasses and now you can see more clearly.

Part II—More Advanced Steps Along the Spiritual Journey

- When you make contact with your true nature (which is God), you are filled with love and generosity for humanity and the entire universe. You are now ready to serve everyone and everything that you come into contact with.

- Life in the outer world really begins when we start to serve others. Once we discover our true calling or vision in life (*dharma*), we serve society through our life mission. Your life mission may be writing poetry, carpentry, gardening, raising children, teaching, building bridges, etc. In this way, your work becomes the expression of your Self. Your visionary work becomes your life and your joy. When we serve humanity through our calling, we transcend our ego and begin to experience God in our self and everything around us.

- As our relationship with our inner God deepens, we realize that we experience less fear and anxiety. The voice of God within us is a constant companion; we do not feel lonely anymore. We become self-entertaining; we drop our judgment and expectations of people.

- As our relationship with God strengthens, we marry our inner truth. Everything we think, say, and do reflects our highest truth. We are no longer interested in impressing others; we lose our sense of self-importance and serve others because our cup is overflowing and we have an abundance of love and joy to share.

- Every day, we meditate on the inner God and receive our daily guidance from the Soul (God). Then we come out of meditation and act on divine guidance. In the spiritual life, we drop society's laws and receive our direction from the *still voice within*.

- When we serve society through our God-given talents, we are filled with abundance. This abundance comes from the richness of our life not necessarily from our material wealth, although material abundance always follows inner abundance.

Characteristics of the Mystic

Most of us associate the term Mystic with enlightened sages of ancient folklore, or someone who has extraordinary powers. By definition, a Mystic is someone who is seeking truth, seeking the One Force which lies beyond intellectual understanding. Hence, as our spiritual journey advances, we too qualify as Mystics. Some of the characteristics associated with a Mystic include being:

- **Autonomous:** The Mystic is independent minded. Guidance comes from within. The Mystic is not motivated by winning the praise and approval of others.
- **Authentic:** The Mystic always tries to listen to and follow his true voice. This is the *Still Voice inside* that I have referred to before.

- **Adaptable:** The Mystic has developed great flexibility; he can tolerate many variations and changes in life and lifestyle.
- **Intuitive:** The Mystic has learned to listen, hear and obey her intuitive guidance.
- **Patient:** Anyone seeking their deepest Self has to be patient. True understanding of the Self takes effort and time.
- **Persistent and Tenacious:** Achieving union (Yoga) with our Soul requires persistent effort and a deep desire to find God. Yoga, meditation, and worship are lifelong activities, not subjects for weekend workshops. As I've mentioned before, meditation is a daily and lifelong endeavor. Mystics are committed to the inner journey.
- **Self-Accepting:** The spiritual aspirant should be kind to herself and accept whatever mental, emotional, and spiritual state she is in at the moment. Wherever you are at, is exactly where you should be now – be humbly grateful.

Experiences During the Spiritual Journey

- When you first begin to meditate, you will have experiences of calmness, deeper concentration, and general happiness regardless of life circumstances. However, these experiences of calmness fade as you enter activity.

- The next stage brings the experience of accessible and deep concentration at will. The Buddhists call this stage *access meditation.* At this stage, you will have deep meditations during most of your sessions. Some of the meditative experiences during this stage are: waves of blissful energy traveling through the body; a sharpening of the five senses; experiencing colors like white, gold, and blue behind the eyelids; hearing divine sounds like chimes and bells. Because meditation accelerates the movement of *Prana* in the body, some meditators feel a sensation likened to ants walking on their skin.

- Once awakened by a realized Master, the dormant *Kundalini* energy moves upward through the spine, piercing through impurities in each of the *chakras*. When this happens, some meditators feel hot flashes traveling up the spine; others experience pain. A feeling of nausea is also common when *Kundalini Shakti* begins her ascent up the spine.

- As *Kundalini* cleanses the heart chakra (*Anahata Chakra*) rises, the spiritual seeker is filled with love and a sense of unity with the entire universe.

- A deeper experience of meditation is when the body, senses and identity of the personality/ego disappear altogether. The meditator dies and becomes the meditation. This is a state of total silence and nothingness. A wide range of psychic powers may appear at this time—visions of past lives, telepathy, telekinesis (moving physical objects with the power of one's mind), clairvoyance, and clairaudience. These powers may distract the meditator from true union with God as such powers tend to create spiritual pride. Be careful of spiritual pride as it eventually retards spiritual progress.

- Still deeper experiences of meditation find the meditator losing the sense of *the Witness*. In other words, there is no body, no mind, no five senses; there is not even a sense of mindfulness watching the process of meditation. Such meditators may have visions of gods, angels, ghosts or violent episodes related to past lives. The experience of these visions is very real to the meditator. An experienced master must lead the aspirant through these stages so that the seeker does not become frightened and withdraw from their practice.

- At the highest states of consciousness, we reach a stage where we experience witnessing the passing of impermanent waves of thought and emotions. We exist in the present moment as a witness; we realize that the body, thoughts and emotions are just impermanent waves of energy—they are not our real self. As the Witness, we realize that our all of life comes from the One Source as Jesus believed, from the One come the many. The freedom of this state is so great that the heart becomes filled with love for all of life and its people. All these emotions happen by themselves, and there is no willpower involved.

- Having realized our Selfless nature as one of pure Spirit (not body, mind and senses), we experience complete spontaneity and transparency. All of life washes through us, and we respond with fluid spontaneity. All judgment and strong opinions disappear. In this stage, we understand that all pain comes from identification with ego, mind and body.

- Finally, the enlightened Being experiences a total release of everything. The more he lets go, the more joyful and enlightened he becomes. All suffering comes from grasping, fear and limited identification with the body, mind, senses and objects of the world.

Important Points To Keep In Mind

- Every stage of meditation and all cycles of consciousness pass and eventually come to an end. Therefore, no matter how blissful a meditative state is, do not hold on to it.

- You can only reach enlightenment by releasing, letting go, and not identifying with any particular spiritual experience.

- An enlightened Being is one who experiences all of life, every spectrum of consciousness during daily life. Such people are capable of being very present and active in daily life.

- Spiritual transformation and experiences can happen any time and anywhere—during meditation, prayer, conversation and even while walking in the street. It is counterproductive to go to a spiritual workshop or retreat expecting an enlightening experience; the more curious and expectant the ego, the farther away you will drift from God. Pay attention to this wonderful Buddhist saying: *God only comes when you are not there.*

Lesson 19

Creative Visualization

Researchers have found that the human mind does not differentiate between material reality and imagined reality. You can actually inspire and motivate your mind to create any reality that you imagine. Creative visualization is the process of using mental imagery to manifest what you want in your life. We have all used this power in our lives without being aware that we are doing it. During this process, you are actually sending visual commands to your subconscious mind so that the subconscious, which is the link between the visible and the quantum world, can mobilize necessary resources to carry out your will.

Though many people use creative visualization on a daily basis, most people use this technique in a reverse or destructive way. Think about all the times you exercise negative thinking to create limitations, anxiety and personal defeat in your daily life. Your mind attracts any circumstance that you constantly think about—just like a magnet! The problem is that your subconscious mind does not care whether you are conceiving something positive or negative. Any and all of your recurring thoughts literally manifest as various positive or negative aspects of your life.

In the practice of creative visualization, imagine everything good that you want in life, in full detail. To practice effective creative visualization, intensely focus on what you want, regularly and with deep concentration. Practice visual imagery in full detail so that you engage your five senses in this practice. See all the colors, shapes, faces, voices, and emotions; visualize everything associated with the joyful circumstance that you want to manifest. I recommend three short, 5-minute visualization sessions per day. Visualization is most effective when the intellectual and rational mind is relaxed, so it is most effective after your daily meditation practices. You can also do your visualizations right before you sleep and immediately after you awaken.

What you visualize may be about any aspect of your life—physical, emotional, financial and spiritual. Experience what you want completely; really feel the event or positive circumstance that you want to manifest.

A very effective technique of creative visualization is to walk around feeling and behaving as though you have already achieved what you want to manifest in life. This method sends a very powerful message to your subconscious mind that you are already on your way to success.

Notice what physical and emotional changes come about as you are visualizing want you really want; the body becomes vitalized and your heart becomes filled with love and joy.

You do not have to have faith in creative visualization for this process to work. Visualization works because a concentrated mind can penetrate the creative subatomic world and stir the God Force to manifest what the mind is focused on. Always practice visualization with a relaxed mind and an open heart.

Vibrational Energy of Visualization

Everything in this universe is made of energy. As mentioned before, in Lesson 5 (The Quantum God), although our five senses perceive everything as matter (solid), at the subatomic level, all matter is pure, invisible, formless energy. Even in atomic physics, scientists have come to know that the tiniest subatomic particles suddenly give way to formless waves.

Every element of our world vibrates at different frequencies. Those elements that vibrate at high frequencies penetrate space deeply and have a powerful influence on the creative God Force. For instance, our flesh and bones are more solid than our thoughts and emotions. The laws of physics tell us that the finer, higher-frequency elements are more powerful and influential than the denser, more solid elements. Therefore, through their high vibrational energy, our thoughts and emotions are able to penetrate space and influence the creative God Force during visualizations; our solid (low energy) physical body does not carry this same ability.

Our thoughts vibrate at very high frequencies. Random thoughts that are scattered and short lived dissipate within a few feet of our body and do not have much impact on our environment. But, when we focus the mind on just one thought, and *emotionalize* that thought, the concentrated thought gains a very high frequency which has a laser-like effect. If the emotions underlying that thought are very powerful, then intensity of the emotions behind the thought make that thought even more powerful. Therefore, emotionalized thoughts influence many others as well as the environment.

When you focus on just one thought and hold it in your mind, that thought magnetizes the environment and organizes the atoms to create exactly the circumstance that you are concentrating on. What this means is that we attract into our lives whatever we think about constantly and at the deepest level.

Your predominant thoughts create every aspect of your life.

You are what you think.

How to Practice Creative Visualization

Before you begin to imagine whatever it is that you want to manifest, it is very important that you relax your mind and body completely.

When you clear the noise in your lower mind (intellect), you will access both the subconscious mind and *Buddhi*. As you will recall from Lesson 15 (The Mind), *Buddhi* is the upper mind, an electromagnetic field just outside the body that has access to all universal information. In order for our mental imagery to be powerful, we need to access the subconscious and upper minds through total mental and physical relaxation. It is also vital to *emotionalize* your imagery. If what you are imagining is important to you, you will naturally stir up and attach powerful emotions to your mental imagery.

Exercise in Visualization

Lie down on your back in a place where you will not be disturbed. Close your eyes and begin relaxing by tuning into your breath. Relax your stomach muscles. As you take slow, rhythmic, deep *Ujjayi* breaths into your stomach, witness the wave-like motions of your breath like a bystander. As you continue to observe your inhalation and exhalation, visualize a gauge with the numbers 0 through 10. The numbers on this gauge show the level of your relaxation; the number 10 reflects resistance and muscle tension, the number 0 indicates total relaxation of your body and emptiness of your mind. With each exhalation, imagine the indicator going down from 10 towards 0. Breathe deeply and slowly; let your mind rock back and forth on the movement of breath.

When your mind is clear and empty, your body relaxed, begin to visualize what you want to manifest in your life. Visualize every detail of what you want in full color— imagine all the faces, shapes, voices, emotions, and circumstances. Allow yourself approximately 5 minutes to visualize the circumstance you want in your life.

Repeat this exercise three times a day. End each visualization session with positive affirmations that support your vision. Remember, affirmations are repetitive positive mental statements and should always be stated in the present tense. Here are some examples:

My life is full of love.

The universe is full of abundance and wealth.

Today I am successful in achieving what is most important.

Lesson 20

Silence

To make contact with our inner God, we need to keep our silence. The whisper of the divine voice is very subtle and at first, difficult to hear unless your mind and speech are still and silent.

To feel our own divinity we need to develop an inward gaze. An inward gaze means we are aware of our inner space and not distracted by outside occurrences. Silence supports an inward gaze whereas excessive noise or talk distracts us from our inward gaze.

The "Sound" of Silence

Pure silence has a profound and beautiful sound; like the sound of the sea when you press a seashell to your ear. Some spiritual seekers hear the sound of silence as a ring that grows louder as they focus more intensely on silence. The sound of silence is in the background, behind all the other sounds around you.

When your mind is restless and busy, take a few deep breaths and focus on the sound of silence. Listening to the hum of silence, you will immediately become present in this moment. When you live in this moment, you are no longer depressed about your past or anxious about your future. There is real joy and lots of energy when we live in this moment.

Create Space for Silence

Even if you have a large family or are parenting young children, create some space in your daily life for silence. The more serious students of meditation take one day or half a day per week to guard their silence as a token of love and respect for their inner God.

In daily life, make an attempt to minimize your words. Excessive talk is truly a sign of restlessness. People who talk a lot use rambling conversations to cover up their inner pain and restlessness. If these people practice daily meditation and maintain some silence every day, their restlessness will eventually fade.

Honestly examine each of your actions and words and modify your words and actions, if necessary, to better support your internal silence. For example, speak in a soft voice; if you are calling someone, get closer to this person and call softly rather than shouting across the room. All your words and the volume at which you speak send out waves and vibrations into your environment. Loud talking or shouting disturbs your silence by releasing very powerful aggressive energy into your environment.

In our daily life, we are constantly bombarded with external sounds that carry angry and aggressive energy. Pay attention to the way loud and aggressive sounds affect your inner silence. Observe the energy you feel next time you hear a car alarm, shrill car horn, piercing telephone ring, loud rap music. Feel the angry and aggressive energy arising from these sounds and sense how it resonates in your body.

Additional Exercises to Support Your Inner Silence

- Sit in an upright position with your head, neck, and spine in vertical alignment. Close your eyes and gently place each thumb on your ears. Begin to listen intensely to the humming sound of silence; it almost sounds like the sea. As you listen intensely, you will notice that all your thoughts and mind noise are dissolving into the inner silence.

- Throughout the day, pay attention to all your actions. When you walk, practice stepping lightly instead of stomping or dragging your feet. When you pick up an object to place it elsewhere, lay it down lightly instead of dropping it.

- If you have a family, arrange to have one meal per week in silence. At first, the children may laugh and mock such an ordeal, silently laugh along with them. Do not resist their playfulness, stay with your breath. Allow everyone around the table to listen to the sound of knife and fork clinking on the dishes. Observe the presence of your loved ones around the table. You will naturally eat more slowly when you eat in silence; you will notice the taste of your food more. You can also send a silent thank you for having abundance in your life. Even if you think you do not have abundance and love around your table at the moment send the prayer of gratitude anyway and notice how you feel after a while.

- If someone tries to engage you in a fight or an argument, guard your silence as you become intensely aware of your breath coming in and breath going out. Keep your silence for some time until the other person becomes more centered. When the other person has calmed down and is more clear minded, you can make your point in a calm and quiet manner. This is the way you can get a point across to people you truly love.

Benefit of Observing Silence

With continued spiritual practice, your entire energy field and all your actions will become more silent and graceful. Your entire Being will emanate pure silence and grace. Your footsteps will become lighter and your speech softer and more kind.

When you practice silence, you will feel that you are becoming more humble and that you are accessing more honest layers of yourself. The whisper of your heart and the voice of your conscious arise from silence; these are the divine aspects of you. In turn, the more you realize your own godliness, the more silent you become. Silence is the language of gods.

Lesson 21

The Power of Thought

You Are What You Think

As mentioned in Lesson 20 (Creative Visualization), all of our thoughts have creative power. Each of our thoughts broadcasts vibratory energy into the atmosphere and influences the subatomic God Force (God) to create the circumstance(s) we are thinking about. The God Force Herself is a thinking force and when we implant our thoughts on this intelligent force, we materialize our predominant thoughts.

You must understand that you create your reality through your own recurring thoughts and beliefs. Your thoughts have a magnetic power to attract whatever circumstances you think about. Those who always worry and obsess about situations they do not want are actually mobilizing forces from inside out to create the very misery they are trying to avoid.

We Live in Our Own Mental Creation

When we identify with our thoughts, we superimpose our mental reality on the reality of the present moment. Through our thoughts, each of us creates a personal reality that we think is the actual reality of the moment. In this way, we experience life through our mental creations and even feel emotional about the fantasy world we have created in our minds. We then spend our entire life collecting evidence to support our personal beliefs about the reality of life.

What Are the Mind and Thoughts?

Our mind and thoughts are really the same. Without thoughts, we have no mind; without a mind, we have no thoughts.

Both our mind and thoughts are constrictions of Pure Consciousness. As mentioned earlier, Pure Consciousness is the silent gap between two thoughts. As long as you live in the silent gap between two thoughts, you are God. Any thought or solution we ever need arises from the silent space between two thoughts—that space of silence is the field of infinite creativity. The minute you identify with one particular thought-bubble, you narrow down the infinite intelligence of Pure Consciousness down to one drop of energy or in this case, one particular thought.

Exercise – Become a Witness

Learn to conserve energy; do not waste your Life Force (*Prana*) by identifying or being entangled with each separate thought. Continually meditate on the silence between two thoughts; meditate on your breath coming in and breath going out; become a witness and master of your rambling mind. Understand that even your scattered thoughts are the dance of consciousness. In fact, everything is the dance of consciousness. When you have incessant thought, just witness the turbulence as the playful dance of consciousness (*Shakti*) that creates the whole universe.

Shakti and Your Mind

The God Force (*Shakti*) is the power and electricity behind our mind and our thoughts. Wherever we direct our mind, *Shakti* follows. If you think about illness all the time, the Life Force (*Shakti*) will energize the notion of illness and bring about illness.

Never obsess or focus your attention on problems; concentrating on problems energizes problems. Instead, focus on the solutions to problems and achievement of your ultimate goal. Do not analyze your negative thoughts and problems. Do not contemplate the cause of your negativity or external problems. Again, by doing so you direct *Shakti* to these problems and energize the very same problems you are trying to avoid!

Free Will

God has given each of us absolute free will. The *Shakti* obeys whatever we choose to believe and think about.

It is very important to understand that God does not care what we create through our thoughts. God gives each of us what we believe in. God is pure, subatomic energy with no judgment or preference; *Shakti* creates whatever we believe in and predominantly think about.

Remember, the God Force simply mirrors your beliefs and thoughts back to you.

The Power to Change Thoughts

Our thoughts are simply waves of energy that arise and dissolve into the ocean of Pure Consciousness—the silent gap between two thoughts.

When we are identified and entangled with each thought, we think that we cannot change our thoughts. This sense of helplessness over our thoughts arises when we lose altitude or distance from the mad river of thoughts rushing through our mind. Both the sense of hopelessness and helplessness are a result of jumping in the rushing river of thought rather than allowing the *Witness* to sit on the shore and just watch the river.

When you sense that the Witness is absent, or you feel powerless over your thoughts, follow the movement of your inhalation and exhalation; soon the *Witness* will return and you will regain a sense of authority over your thoughts. As you continue to watch your relationship with your thoughts you will soon realize that although you cannot forcefully eliminate negative thoughts, you can always replace negative thoughts with positive ones once you become aware of negative thinking. Only one thought can occupy your mind at any one time, so, why choose a negative thought?

Through continued meditation, we gain altitude and become liberated from the incessant rise and fall of individual thoughts. Once we gain this awareness and altitude over thought-bubbles, we have acquired mastery of the mind. The ability to witness and become aware of our thoughts is what I call real freedom.

You have the power to replace any thought as soon as it arises. Work on catching negative thoughts at the very first impulse. At that point, there is very little energy behind the negative thought. Catch the very first impulse of negativity and replace negative thoughts with positive thoughts. It is just that simple! If you obsess about negative thoughts or analyze them, that first negative wave of thought will multiply into hundreds of negative thought-bubbles within a few minutes.

The exercise to gain elevation over our thoughts and replace negative thoughts with positive thoughts is continuous. Do not give up. No matter how many times you have to replace the recurring thought or reestablish your sense of Witness, know that your persistence will pay off. Remember that your oldest mental habits (*samskaras*) are the most stubborn and have established residency in your subconscious, a position they will not readily relinquish. As a result of our *samskaras* rooting themselves so firmly in our subconscious, we have unconsciously become addicted to our repetitive negative thought patterns. For instance, I know many people who actually like thinking and worrying about their problems—they have become very familiar and friendly with their anxiety and depression. These people have grown used to worry and anxiety and actually feel incomplete if they are not anxious or depressed. The good news is that with dedication and concentration, you can choose and change your thoughts.

When Life is Hard

Anyone can feel good and think positive thoughts when life is comfortable and trouble-free. When big obstacles appear in our lives, the mind has a strong tendency to cling to the negative. During the difficult times, make twice the effort to replace negative thoughts with positive thoughts.

God will not make the effort for you. You must develop and apply willpower and inner strength to regularly practice positive thinking. Make positive thinking part of your spiritual practice.

The Power of Prayer and Gratitude

It does not matter what we pray for and how we ask for it, what matters is that we believe that we will receive what we are praying for. We will not receive what we ask for, rather, we will receive what we believe in. A person may ask God for wealth but deeply believe that he will remain poor. In the above case, it would be impossible for the God Force to manifest something if you yourself do not believe in that reality.

The God Force gives us exactly what we believe in. Jesus Christ said, *whatsoever you desire, when you pray, believe that you will receive it, and you shall have it.*

Gratitude is a very powerful energy. When we are grateful for what we have, we energize the notion that we are God and that we are connected to the Source of all creation and infinite abundance. Gratitude is a prayer in itself that reinforces the belief that we are worthy and that our life is filled with abundance.

Lesson 22

The Spiritual Laws of Nature

To master the art of joyful living, we must understand and cooperate with the spiritual laws of nature. If we observe these laws in our daily life, we will live more harmoniously with nature and experience a kinder, easier life. In this lesson, we will review the most fundamental natural laws.

Law of Action and Reaction

All your thoughts, words and actions broadcast vibratory energy into space and create waves that boomerang right back to you. Whenever you take action, nature returns the same energy back to you as an equivalent reaction; hence, the old adage, *as you sow, so shall you reap.* Anger begets anger, laughter brings laughter, love returns love. Look around you; everything presently in your life is mirroring your deep beliefs and consequences of your prior actions back to you.

Law of Giving and Receiving

All of nature maintains a balance between giving and receiving. For example, the sea gives vapor to a cloud; clouds, in turn, give themselves to rain; rain gives itself to a watermelon patch; the watermelon gives itself to us; we plant trees; the leaves from the tree give vapor back to the cloud, and the cloud drips back into the sea. The cycle of giving and receiving perpetuates itself in this way. Examine the cycle of giving and receiving in your own life. If you give a lot but are not able to receive, you grow tired, angry and bitter. If you only receive and are not able to give back, your friends will leave you and you will feel isolated.

Law of Constant Change

The subatomic God Force is constantly in flux. Everything in life is constantly changing and reforming itself because this is what the God Force does within the Unified Field of creation. Even our own body, as a manifestation of God, completely regenerates itself every two years. Imagine, every cell, molecule and bone in your body is completely renewed every two years! If you focus on the waves of energy and sensations in your inner body, you will notice that nothing is permanent; all sensations within your subatomic body such as pain, itching or cramps are always changing and in flux. What we call "I" is nothing but an energetic body of fluctuating waves.

Never cling to the passing moment; you will be violating natural law; life will pass you by as you try to fixate on time and circumstances. Nothing ever stands still, not even your close relationships. Be courageous, expect change, welcome it, and adapt to changes.

Law of Energy and Chaos

The one and only creative energy in the universe is the God Force (*Shakti*). Divine Energy cannot be destroyed; the total amount of *Shakti* (Life Force) always remains the same, though it may change form. For instance, we can take a newspaper and burn it, and the changed form which results in heat, fire, and ashes, will amount to the same net amount of energy as that which was contained in the original newspaper. We can change patterns of energy but the net amount of energy always remains the same. Most human beings do not create new energy; they simply reorganize the present amount of energy flowing in our atmosphere into different forms.

In our universe, energy is always shifting and swirling in chaotic patterns. Chaos is not dangerous, because chaos is how the God Force creates everything. The God Force moves in seemingly chaotic patterns and regularly reshapes itself into new forms of life.

Chaos is what we experience as the unknown. Our ego, mind and five senses are very frightened of the unknown, but the spiritual path demands that we enter the unknown in a state of trust and faith. Every time we dive into deep meditation, we are exploring unknown parts of ourselves.

The secret of an enlightened person is *energy management.* In daily life, learn to distribute your Life Force in directions that fulfill the requirements of your life. Know this— a joyful, successful life requires energy management. Meditation increases your awareness of subtle energies in your body; with microscopic awareness, you can detect where your Life Force is traveling.

Notice what elements are draining you and what life factors are nourishing your vital energies. Once you become energy-aware, you can manage your Life Force much more effectively by sticking to the most important priorities instead of being lost in endless distractions.

Law of Inwardness (Power of Subtlety)

God is the subatomic energy of consciousness. This energy is very subtle due to its refined, ultra-high frequency that vibrates above one million cycles per second. The God Force manifests itself into numerous shapes and sizes. Grosser manifestations of the God Force are dense; the denser an object, the lower its energy field based on its slower vibrational frequency.

Our subtle inner body is an enormous powerhouse. If we can focus our mind inwardly and identify with subtle wave-like energies pulsating in the inner body, rather than our solid flesh and bones, we will magnetize our entire body with the ultra-high vibrations of the God Force (*Shakti*).

Law of Cycles

All of life moves in cycles. The moon changes in cycles, the four seasons trade places, there is a repetitive pattern in the ebb and flow of waves, human life itself is a cycle of birth and death. Realizing that everything in life has distinct phases that are part of a larger cycle helps us understand that no episode of life is permanent.

Whatever is occurring in your life right now, know that this is only a phase or season—it will soon pass. There are phases appropriate for taking actions. During other phases, you should pause, reflect and plan. When your awareness becomes refined through meditation, you will intuitively know the time for starting a project and the time for rest and reflection.

Law of Balance

Everything in nature strives to regain balance. For example: the tree swaying in the wind; the bird sitting on a wire: your sick body on its way to recovery: the earth after a volcanic eruption, earthquake or storm. All of these are examples of natural elements regaining their natural balance.

Just as nature continuously strives to regain balance, we must work toward establishing balance in our lives. There are several different aspects of our life that require balancing. For example, there is the mental and emotional balance, the balance between rest and activity, and the balance between spiritual and material life. Meditation and spiritual practice help us regain and maintain balance in all aspects of our lives.

Meditation and breath awareness help us steady the mind. As we endeavor toward balance by calming the mind, those who are even-tempered will make faster spiritual progress. As you learn to witness ever-changing thoughts and emotions, instead of identifying with them, you will become more balanced and steadier in your joy, happiness, and progress.

Law of Oneness and Inter-Relationship

All of life is interconnected. There is no such thing as being out of relationship with people and other elements of our universe. Only the human ego thinks it is separate from the rest.

The entire universe is made up of one energy—the energy of consciousness. We are all made of the same undifferentiated energy, therefore we are all one. Everything we think, do and say flows outward in waves and impacts others. Similarly, what others think, do, and say directly affects us.

The truly spiritual Being has learnt the art of living well—how to optimize personal fulfillment while also contributing the most to her society and environment. The spiritual Being feels the interdependency of the universe.

Law of Least Resistance

When you observe nature you will notice that everything in nature flows through the path of least resistance and least effort. As with the other spiritual laws explored in this lesson, we can learn a lot from nature. Just as nature chooses the path of least resistance and effort, so should our life. You have the option of relaxing into life and trusting the flow of the moment, while remaining very active. For example, sometimes you may feel lonely and strongly feel the need for a relationship, but that companion is nowhere to be seen. When nature seems to close one door, stay awake and aware of what the moment brings; find the path of least resistance and trust that something good is cooking out there. Stay with your breath and actively work with the moment instead of fighting the moment.

This concept of going with the flow is not the same as laziness or apathy. Play the game of life fully; give 500 percent of yourself, but do not choose directions that meet with natural resistance, or those that violate the truth of your heart and Soul. Do not make decisions that your very Soul and body resist. Take the path that most naturally comes to you; this is your *dharma*. d*harma* is your life-calling which is naturally in line with your God-given talents and natural tendencies.

Through meditation and other spiritual practices that increase your awareness of the inner body, you will literally feel any violation of your Soul and your heart's desire in your physical body. When you make an unnatural decision, you will sense your heart racing, shallowness of breath, perspiration on your palms, headaches, muscle tension, backaches, and anxiety in the stomach area, etc. Pay attention to these physical sensations and the choices that triggered them.

Law of Two Basic Emotions—Love and Fear

The two principle emotions in the universe are love and fear. All other emotions come from these two primary emotions. Love is the sensation of the Soul; fear is the sensation of the ego. Fear cannot possibly exist in the presence of love. Through love we feel expanded and limitless, through fear we feel constricted and helpless. Through love we experience the spiritual certainty that *the more I give, the more I will receive.* The more you love, the more expanded and courageous you feel.

When we make decisions out of fear, nature returns the same negative and fearful reaction back to us. When we act out of love, the same positive energy comes back to us.

Law of Choice

At any given moment, we face choices in our lives. The God Force will not interfere with our free will. Thus, as we make decisions at any junction in our life, we must follow through and gladly take responsibility for those decisions. The God Force will accept our will and mirror the appropriate response back to us.

God is spiritual energy and every choice we make broadcasts its own unique energy into space. In any given situation, we have the choice to select a loving response or a fearful response. Remember, the strongest spiritual electricity radiates out of love. Try to make choices rooted in love.

Whatever choice we make, we must fully accept responsibility for our choices. This is the sign of a mature spiritual person. Too many of us constantly blame others for our own choices. By blaming others we succumb to fear, de-energize ourselves and perpetuate a sense of feeling victimized. Since the God Force will not interfere with your free will, as long as you choose victimhood, you will remain a victim.

Law of Intention and Attention

Every thought, word and action originates from a seed of intention or purpose. The same action performed with two different intentions will carry two very different energies and will impact the world differently. Be aware of your underlying intentions; those intentions that will harm others will also cause you suffering. The God Force does not differentiate between the energy we intend for others and that which we intend for ourselves. Therefore, the seed intention of our thoughts, words and actions determines our own experience.

After you clarify your intent, put your attention on your intention. Whatever you put your attention on will grow, strengthen, and prosper.

Law of Expectations

Expectations reduce our joy in the present moment. If you want to live fully and joyously, drop your expectations and live in the present moment, detached from expectation of gains or final outcomes. Make your very best effort, play the game fully in the moment, then, leave the rest up to the God Force.

Law of the Present Moment

The only reality is the present moment—the past is long gone, and most people know nothing about the future. Always strive to be fully aware of the present moment. As soon as you become entangled with your thoughts and emotions, you lose contact with the present moment.

The two best techniques for living in the moment are breath awareness, and awareness of all physical sensations within your body.

Law of *Dharma*

Every human being is born with one unique set of God-given talents that no one else can quite duplicate. Find your God-given talent (*dharma*), and make that your calling, your commitment to God. When you live out your *dharma*, working and playing are the same; you will receive vital energy even while you are working. Living your *dharma* is the true way to success and happiness.

Law of Detachment

The Buddha said attachment to anything is the source of pain. As soon as we identify with an external object or event, we lose contact with our inner God. When we lose contact with *Shakti* within, we lose our internal Life Force to something outside of ourselves. Throughout the day, keep your focus within—concentrate on your breath coming in, breath going out; chant the mantra *"Aum"*; or simply talk to your inner God.

On all projects, do your very best but do not be attached to the gains or outcome; place the decision for the outcome in the hands of God. This is not the same concept as apathy or laziness. Detachment is the opposite of emotional obsession. Never be attached to anything outside of your inner God. Before taking on any project, ask yourself, *how can I please God with this task?* Then, perform your action and move onward with the next moment. Release the results of your efforts to God and nature; let them take care of the results.

Law of Opposites

The God Force has created everything in opposites. For every element or energy, the opposite also coexists. For example: good/bad, light/dark, poverty/wealth, birth/death, etc. This is the nature of the God Force. Do not think that birth is better than death. All opposites are part of a natural life.

The Quantum Law – the Smaller the More Powerful

In the material world, the bigger is the more powerful. In the subatomic world of the Spirit, the smaller, subtle forces are the most powerful.

A prime example of the power of small forces is the atomic bomb. Imagine, six million atoms can fit on the tip of a needle. Splitting of these minute particles is what destroyed the Japanese cities of Hiroshima and Nagasaki in mere minutes. See how powerful small forces are!

Now, turn this example inward and examine how your most subtle negativities are the ones that control your behavior the most. Through continued practice of meditation, *Pranayama* (breath control), and other spiritual exercises, your awareness will become more subtle and refined. You will develop microscopic radar that can tune into the tiniest waves of energy. This is where the real power lies, within the most minuscule waves of the Life Force.

When you develop the capability to detect and manage your most subtle thoughts, emotions, and energy waves, you will be the master of your own life.

Lesson 23

How to Experience Truth

You can only experience truth when your mind is very still and your heart is open. When you step into this moment without superimposing your old beliefs on the NOW, you experience the immensity of life unfolding before you.

Truth Is Not Thought

We can never experience truth through thought because all our thoughts are conditioned by past experiences or worries about the future. The past is already gone and the subatomic God Force only creates reality in this instant. What happens when we operate from our limited mind is that the mind forms thoughts based on past experiences. We then carry those past experiences and memories into the present moment through our perceptions and old beliefs. When we superimpose our mental conditioning on present moment reality, we do not grasp the truth or reality of life as it is right now—we see only what we want to see through a mind conditioned by the past.

Furthermore, by superimposing our past mental conditioning on the present moment, we forcefully create situations (through our past beliefs) that make today seem like our past. As we continue to superimpose past experiences and perceptions on the "here and now", we unconsciously influence our present behavior so as to create a rigid and stale future incarcerated in the tomb of our limited thinking. Of course, the reality is that every moment is absolutely fresh and new. Since our ego and mind resist any change and stepping into the unknown, these parts of us always resist a naïve and unguarded acceptance of whatever the moment brings.

Experiencing God in everything, seeing the essential truth in everything, also means not being entangled in passing thoughts but continuously stepping into that gap between two thoughts.

Emphasize Feeling Over Thought

Your feeling body is always a more accurate gauge of reality than your thinking mind. Try to feel more than you think—feeling is different from thinking. Simply remain empty, open and thoughtless, and through that total presence, emptiness, and openness, you will experience the essence and truth of life. Should the need come about for problem-solving and creativity, these will spontaneously arise from Pure Consciousness, the gap between two thoughts.

Stepping Into the Unknown

The nature of mind and ego is to cling to the familiar, to the known. Unfortunately, we can never directly experience or learn anything new about life through what is already known to others; we must be attuned and open to today in order to learn our own truth. The sciences and history have accumulated many facts. It is okay for us to use this accumulated knowledge in order not to reinvent the wheel, but we must understand that we will not discover our own truth, calling, and ingenuity through what has already been experienced by others.

Everything you already know is the result of past conditioning. Think about what I am saying; your entire education and social/ cultural conditioning comes from past knowledge -- what is already known. These are all other people's thoughts, not your own unique experience and ingenuity.

The spiritual mind knows that true learning comes from stepping into the unknown which exists in the unguarded, unexpected moment. We must go beyond the intellectual and subconscious mind which is already conditioned by past experience. Whenever we step into fresh territory, the unknown, we feel excited, vibrant and energetic. If there is a part of you that is scared and holding back, be sure it is your ego and mind wanting to cling to the familiar.

There is Power in Admitting "I Don't Know"

Through meditation and other spiritual practices, we de-condition the mind; we free the mind from its past conditioning beliefs based on past experiences. Experience of the true Self (Soul) through meditation makes us humble and we gradually find that we are willing to admit that we don't know what will happen today. Openly admitting "I don't know" is a very powerful experience. Practice stepping into the unknown territories of life and staying connected with the feeling that you really do not know what is going to happen next in your life. Take a day off and wander through the day one moment to the next, not planning, not knowing what will come next. Just embrace, absorb, and work with whatever comes. This is how you accumulate your own knowledge and truth.

The mind that openly admits, "I do not know", is open to unlimited discoveries. Put aside all your books, your encyclopedias, the meditation masters and the sayings of the holy prophets. Unburden your mind and empty all the known facts. As you tap into that vast space of emptiness, remain innocent and unguarded; pay attention to the "here and now", and you will come into contact with enormous insights. Insight means immediate perception without any mental analysis. When the mind is still and unfolding every moment there is no end to learning and insight.

The Difference Between Concentration and Attention

When we concentrate the mind on one point, we essentially exclude the rest of life; we cut out the periphery through single-pointed concentration. In the beginning of spiritual practice, the Guide encourages you to develop single-pointed concentration as a way of quieting the wild mind so you can dive deeper into yourself. Later, as the mind becomes more silent, you can remain totally empty, vast and capable of grasping a wider reality in the present moment. This mindful awareness (attention) of everything "here and now" is a state of total de-concentration instead of narrow concentration.

The student of meditation naturally progresses from concentration to mindful awareness and attention. As concentration becomes laser-like suddenly a huge vacuum of nothingness opens up and concentration melts into attention and awareness of "what is".

Attention is complete, silent and open observation of everything that goes on in this moment without focusing on just one narrow topic. This is the difference between concentration and attention; while concentration refers to narrowing down, attention refers to opening up to everything. We can expand our life experience through absolute attention (mindfulness) to present moment reality. In this sense, attention means staying awake and alert to our surroundings.

Attention is the act of being present and fully aware of our surroundings without categorizing, labeling, or mentally analyzing what goes on around us. If you stop by a rose bush and your mind starts to verbalize, *this is a rose bush*, you have already missed the essence or truth of the rose. But if you remain attentive and open without any mental analysis or recall of other roses, this rose will totally envelop and transform you.

When you are here, in the NOW, with complete attention, your mind will constantly unfold and learn new things.

The Difference Between Intellect and Intelligence

Intellect is the functioning of thought without emotion—it is the brain without the heart. Developing intellect does not make us intelligent. Real intelligence is a perfect unification of mind and heart.

Intellect cannot solve our biggest problems because mind and intellect are limited to thought. Our thoughts are limited by what we already know from past experience.

Pure Consciousness, the silent gap between two thoughts, is the Source of all thoughts, memory and creativity. We can access Pure Consciousness when the mind is very still. Movement in the vast ocean of consciousness creates tiny waves which we experience as waves of thought. *Maya,* the big illusion, is that we then take one of these waves (thoughts) in the ocean of consciousness and we say, *look, look that thought is me; that is my personality!*

Through intelligence, the harmony between heart and mind, we are able to feel life deeply. Not only do we understand many facts (intellect), but our heart is also open to the love of life. When we remain unguarded, present and mentally still, all of life moves through us and we feel enormous energy, compassion and love--this is real intelligence.

Ego and Intellect – Barriers to Truth

The life of ego and the mind are complicated. The nature of ego and mind is to create an endless array of problems and illusions. Each time you solve one problem for the mind and ego these two respond by inventing more fantasies and problems which take you further from your inner truth. Mind and ego have the power to create constant illusions. As long as you are identified and attached to these parts of yourself, you will experience complications and pain. The more egoless you become, the simpler your life becomes.

Mental analysis of life, arising from ego and mind, separates us from the full experience of life. One of our most powerful emotional defenses is analyzing life instead of living it fully. When we learn to live in the silence between thoughts, we are in touch with the beauty and simplicity of life in this moment; we feel lightness, joy and energy and are able to live life fully; we are rooted in truth.

How to Experience Truth

Most of us at some point have confused our search for intellectual knowledge as our search for truth. The reality is that knowledge in the form of external facts often complicates our inner pursuit of truth. Many people study numerous books, follow the news on television and conduct research on the Internet in their search for knowledge. Through constant feeding of their intellects, people call themselves *intellectuals*. While culturally, most countries place emphasis on acquiring intellectual knowledge, the result of internalizing accumulated facts is that most people have little idea about who they are and what their own truth is. Most of the students I initially work with struggle for weeks to give me a list of their core values and their top five priorities in life. Ninety percent of most people's intellect is made up of other people's ideas and priorities. This kind of intellectual activity creates mediocrity because pure intellectualization overshadows emotional intelligence, intuition and creativity. True artists and creators create mental space; they create sweet solitude for themselves. Through this open space, they are able to experience their inner truth and allow original ideas to spring forth.

In order to experience truth, we must break down all of our mental habits and conditioned preconceptions of life. We must train ourselves to be aware of all that goes on around us in the moment. Infinite knowledge and truth lie at the edge of all thought. Remember, we experience Pure Consciousness when we are thoughtless. When thought becomes still, even for a second, we experience vast insight and unending knowledge. When thought ceases, we experience truth.

Lesson 24

Intuition

Intuition is what we call the Sixth Sense in the spiritual realm. Everyone has intuitive power, but not everyone is open to receiving intuitive guidance. Once you train your intuition, your Sixth Sense can provide you with instantaneous solutions in any situation where you need assistance.

Intuition represents our higher intelligence. It arises from the *Buddhi* or the higher mind. We can access *Buddhi* when we are physically relaxed and have emptied our mind chatter as much as possible.

Intuition does not speak to us in plain language. Most of the time, intuition communicates with us through dreams, symbols, books, incidents, or a person who happens to say something which is the answer to our question.

The Difference Between Ego and Intuition

The voice of intuition sounds different from the voice of ego. Ego's voice is nagging and loud and its demands are based on fear; ego does not trust in the flow of life nor recognize the present moment. When you listen to the voice of ego, you feel pressured to carry out its demand. When you act in response to ego any sense of satisfaction or gratification are temporary and do not last.

In contrast, the intuitive voice of guidance is soft, loving, non-judgmental, and sporadically persists until you take notice. The voice of intuition is like a faint whisper that does not insist.

When you think about accepting intuitive advice, you feel empowered, joyful, and optimistic about following your hunch. When you act in accordance with intuition, you experience a deep sense of contentment and fulfillment.

From childhood, we have systematically been taught to develop our sense of ego or "I-ness". We have been trained to edit our intuition using logic. This is especially true for boys and men. Females are less criticized for being intuitive and listening to spontaneous emotions that arise out of intuition. The result of a very logical and analytical upbringing is that we learn to ignore our inner voice for so long, we barely hear it or confuse this voice of guidance with senseless mind noise or ego based thoughts.

The Difference Between Intellect and Intuition

Intuition is different from intellect. Intellect is linear logic; it takes our intellectual mind multiple rational steps before it can find a solution.

Intuitive information appears in a flash; the insight seems to jump out at us from nowhere. That "nowhere" or field of emptiness is where insights and innovation come from; it is the field of Pure Consciousness where all of creation is born. Einstein called this field of Pure Consciousness, *The Unified Field.*

Intellect is useful in carrying out the hunches or insights that we receive from our intuition, but intellectual power is very limited as compared to intuitive power. Put your intellect in the service of your intuition. Use your intellect to carry out the guidance that you receive through intuitive insight.

Three Types of Intuition

Tuning into our Sixth Sense is following our intuition. Most people receive the message of their Sixth Sense in these ways:

Thoughts

Sometimes an intuitive thought will suddenly come to you out of nowhere. This kind of thought is very different from rational or logical thought. Intuitive thought is like a thought you did not ask for. You simply "know" something instantly and with a sense of certainty, but do not discern how you know this information – it suddenly flashes on the screen of your mind.

Emotions

Other times you will have a hunch or intuitive feeling about something. This is traditionally called *woman's intuition*. In America, they also use the expression *I feel it in my gut*. Through emotional intuition you cannot only tap into your own thoughts and feelings, but can also detect other people's thoughts and feelings. Emotional intuition enables you to walk into a room and immediately sense other people's emotional energy.

Physical

There are other times when you physically feel intuition in your body. For example, you might sense a worrisome feeling in your stomach, or feel fear-based intuition in your heart. Another example of physical intuition is when you feel your muscles tense up when you are about to make a wrong decision.

Developing Our Intuitive Power

Since most of us have negated our intuition for many years, it is important to pay close attention to the way we access and receive information from our Sixth Sense. Just as we exercise our muscles, we must exercise our intuitive power before we can fully rely on our intuition. Carefully witness your intuitive thoughts, emotions and physical sensations and use these observations to train your intuitive power.

How to Access Intuition

Before you ask for intuitive advice, it is important to quiet your environment. Unplug the telephone and turn off the television or stereo; find a room where you will not be disturbed.

Relax; take 15 deep breaths into your stomach. With every exhalation release all the tension in your body. Also with each exhalation, release your mind chatter; imagine that your mind chatter is coming out of your nostrils with each outgoing breath. Now, ask your intuition a question. Do not get agitated if the answer is not immediate. Maintain your sense of calm and simply trust the answer will materialize when you are ready to receive it. The answer will come to you sooner or later, when you are in a state of emptiness and deep relaxation.

Below are a few more specific exercises for accessing your intuition. Remember to be patient with yourself. The answers will come, in some way, shape or form, sometimes when you least expect it.

Exercise One: Receiving "Yes/No" answers

Imagine a life-situation where you need to know a "yes" or "no" answer to an important question. First, completely understand your question and make sure your question can be answered with a "yes" or "no" response.

Sit with your head, neck and spine in vertical alignment. Close your eyes and relax. Take several deep breaths into your stomach. With each exhalation, release all your body tension and your thoughts.

When you are totally relaxed, open the palm of your hands and imagine that you are receiving the word "yes" in one of your hands, and the word "no" in your other hand.

Now, ask your Sixth Sense your important question. How does each hand feel? Pay close attention to all the sensations and feelings that you sense in your hands.

There are no absolute rules in terms of what kind of intuitive answer you should receive or how your hands should feel. Each person will receive their answer in a different way. Take as much time as you like with this exercise. It is important not to try too hard; trying to access intuition only makes you tense and closes the channels to your higher mind.

Also, let go of any analytical thinking. Your analytic mind (intellect) has absolutely no intuitive power. When you try hard or over-analyze the results of your intuition exercises, you are actually sending a message to your mind and to the universe that you do not trust the power of intuition. Lack of faith and our ego always keep the God Force away.

Exercise Two: Choosing the Right Path

Use this exercise when you have to choose one path amongst several alternatives.

First, clarify in your mind each of your alternatives. Next, mentally imagine each of your alternatives as a different path or road. Now, relax with deep breathing and totally release all muscular tension and thoughts with each exhalation.

With a relaxed body and empty mind, imagine yourself walking down each of these roads. While traveling down each road, notice all the images, symbols, bodily sensations and emotions that you experience. Typically, when you are visualizing your walk down the right path your body will feel energized, your heart open and loving, and your mind optimistic.

Take your time with this exercise. Let yourself experience everything in a state of total relaxation and emptiness. When you come out of this meditation, write down or note your experiences in your spiritual journal. Write in a free flow of thought; resist the temptation to mentally analyze or judge what you experienced.

Exercise Three—Walking into an Unknown, Future Event

In this exercise, you will receive guidance about a future event in your life. Make sure you have at least 20 minutes for this exercise. Choose a room or space where you will not be disturbed.

Like the previous two exercises, begin by closing your eyes and totally relaxing your mind and body through deep breathing. When you are empty of thought and totally relaxed, imagine yourself walking into that future event in your life. See all the details and symbols that come to your mind. For example, visualize the room, the lighting, the faces of other people, what they are wearing, saying, etc.

Focus on what you want to accomplish during this future event. Also, focus on your feelings, emotions and moods during the entire visualization. Observe what happens to you throughout the visualization of this future event.

At the end of this visualization, imagine you are talking to a Sage. If you noticed any faults or difficulties in the way the future event took shape, empty yourself with a few outgoing breaths and then ask the Sage to suggest how you can improve the future outcome.

Obstacles to Accessing Intuition

The biggest obstacle blocking our intuition is fear. Fear takes us out of a state of mental relaxation and brings us back to intellectual analysis which has no intuitive power.

In the beginning, it is very difficult to trust intuition. Start with small steps. For example, call a friend who keeps coming into your mind, visit a place that you want to visit, or take a different road to your workplace. The easiest exercise to help develop your confidence in your intuitive power is the "yes" or "no" exercise described above.

As you continue to develop your sense of intuition you will need to discern between ego and intuition. There are three ways of knowing if the advice coming to you is from intuition and not the ego:

1. You can feel intuitive guidance in your body. Intuitive advice relaxes your body and deepens your breath. Counter-intuitive action tenses your muscles and your breathing becomes short and erratic because your body intuitively feels like it is a burden to go against its own intuition.

2. Intuitive advice is persistent. Your Sixth Sense will continue to sporadically send you hunches or messages.

3. Following intuition will make you energetic, joyful, and alive. You will feel love and compassion in your heart. The power of universal energy will flow through you when you follow your intuition.

How to Interpret the Advice of Your Intuition

Sometimes you will ask for intuitive advice and receive an answer but feel like you are mentally and rationally inventing the answer. That is alright; in the beginning, just continue to relax and empty yourself with your outgoing breath. Every day, ask your intuition for more guidance and carefully note the very first image, word, feeling or sense you have during your practice. The more you listen to your intuition, the more She speaks to you. After a while, you will establish a constant connection with your genuine intuitive power.

Be careful about jumping to quick conclusions about messages or symbols that your Sixth Sense sends you. Just watch the images and do not force yourself to decipher the meanings. The meanings will intuitively come to you when you are totally relaxed and empty. Over time and with practice, your intuitive sense will mature, and you will know if you are forcing a hasty conclusion about the meaning of symbols and messages that you receive during intuition exercises.

Be very patient about establishing contact with your intuition. Each time you ask for advice, first go into deep relaxation. Then empty your mind of all thought and prepare to openly receive answers, symbols or images without judgment or mental analysis. After you receive guidance from your Sixth Sense, be aware of what actually happens in your everyday life. Keep your eyes open as you track the everyday events and compare them to the intuitive advice that you received from your Sixth Sense.

The Importance of Practice

Remember, just as we exercise to strengthen our physical body, we must also regularly exercise our intuitive powers.

In the beginning, you may feel very uncomfortable about asking for intuitive advice. As you continue practicing intuition, your confidence will increase enabling you to ask more direct questions and better hear your intuitive voice.

Following your intuition may not win you any applause from old friends. On the contrary, it may arouse negative judgment in others because following your inner voice is an end to mindless compromise, socializing and being influenced by the opinions of others. Continue with your practice regardless of how others respond to your newfound insight and direction. Your practice will significantly enhance your confidence in yourself.

As you follow your intuition, your life will become more joyful and your sense of aliveness and personal energy will increase.

Lesson 25

Inviting the Presence of God

The God Force is always flowing and circulating in the space all around us as well as in the inner space within our body.

There are times in our life when we fall into the illusion that God has forgotten us. This is an illusion because God is actually a subatomic energy of consciousness that is ever-present everywhere, even in the atoms within our cells and molecules, as well as in the empty space surrounding you right now (Lesson 6, Space - The House of God).

During periods of doubt and faithlessness in our lives, it is we who lose our subtle awareness of the God Force circulating within and right outside in the periphery of our body. Because the God Force so completely envelops us we often cannot distinguish its presence.

Imagine if you ask a fish *what is water?* What answer do you think a fish will give? The fish will probably have no idea what you are talking about; a fish is born in water, breaths through water, and sustains its life in water, how can it stand apart from water and know that fish are different from water? Use this same analogy for yourself— the God Force is so completely in and around you that although you have never seen or been anything but God, you probably do not realize that you are in God's embrace right now. Just as water permeates the life of a fish, the God Force totally permeates and envelops you, your life, and the universe.

The God Force never leaves us. What blocks our awareness of the Divine energy is always the same two obstacles—our ego and our chattering mind. There is a very thin veil separating us from God. The second our mind becomes still and there are no thoughts, we feel the presence of God in the present moment.

What Does the Presence of God Feel Like?

The energy of God is Pure Consciousness, that state of non-thought where awareness and deep attention exist. To the ego/personality the energy of consciousness, or the Witness, feels like the presence of another person in a pitch-dark room. If you were to stand in a pitch dark room you might be able to sense another presence, but you would be hard pressed to prove through your five senses that there was indeed Someone there, calmly watching.

When our mind is totally silent and we exist in this very moment, we feel that all of space, outside and inside our body, is alive with a kind of Presence that knows us intimately, and it also knows when we are focused on it; the God Force is aware that we are aware of it.

Anyone who has experienced the presence of God will say that this experience is beyond time, space, emotions, beliefs, expectations and human words. Moreover, each person experiences the presence of God in a totally unique way. What is not unique is the fact that experiencing the presence of God transforms our lives and opens our hearts.

When we come into the presence of God, all our fears dissolve and we feel expanded, without any personal boundaries. Each time we contact God, we become more loving, calm and content with the simple things in life. Being in the presence of God does not eliminate our life problems, but it does change how we perceive the same life situation. Because our fears and defenses dissolve, we become more accepting of others' faults and we develop compassion even for violent and hateful people.

Each time we feel the presence of God, it is a new experience. We never experience the God Force the same way because the subatomic God Force is fluid and ever changing. While the subatomic God Force may constantly change, the presence of God (energy of consciousness) is unchanging and timeless; it is the same God that has existed for millions of years. Although the material world is always changing, the one Source of all matter (God living beneath the atom) is unchanging and always the same. We can always go home to God, knowing that God is there waiting.

Exercise —"I AM THAT"

In order to feel the vibrational energy of the God Force around you, close your eyes and relax yourself with deep, long, rhythmic *Ujjayi* breaths. With each exhalation, loosen your muscles. With each outgoing breath, allow all thoughts to rush out of your mind, through your nostrils.

Now, visualize a bluish/purple light (cobalt-blue color) enveloping your entire body and extending a distance of about 1 meter away from your body. This area and color of light encompasses your Soul. With your eyes closed, send a lot of love outward to your Soul. While visualizing the cobalt-blue-colored light around your body, draw that light into your heart with each inhalation. With each exhalation, send the violet light of your Soul inward to all your cells and molecules. Now inhaling, mentally repeat the words: I AM THAT, I AM THAT, I AM THAT...

Lesson 26

Prayer

Meditation is the process of realizing that we are gods; prayer is the act of contacting and requesting something from God.

When we first begin to pray, it is usually out of pain. This human pain is always based on the conflict between our isolated ego and our heart's desire to be one with God. At the deepest level, we all want to know that God distinguishes us as an individual and cares about each of us individually. Thus, our heart cries out in prayer, *God I need your help, I need you, I feel so alone, please help me.*

Prayer is the Worship of Our Inner God

As our prayers and meditation deepen, we begin to 'feel' the presence of God within and all around us. Prayer in the spiritual sense is the worship of our inner God. Since God is everywhere evenly present, including within us, worship of God is actually deep love for the entire universe as well as worship of our Self (Soul).

Through deep and sincere prayer, we merge and become one with God. What begins as prayer to an "outside" God for help ends with the realization that, *I am the same divine God Force that creates this universe.* Thus, the advanced student prays to honor and worship the Self, not an entity outside of the Self.

Deep Prayer is a Very Private Act

Sincere and powerful prayer happens when we create a private and solitary communion with God. Deep prayer is a very private act. When we publicly discuss our prayers and the answers to our prayers, we weaken the power of our prayer. Cherish your relationship with God as a very private relationship.

Prayer Is An Act of Surrender and Humility

Prayer is an act of surrender—surrendering our willpower and ego to a Higher Force (God). The act of surrendering the ego is very important because through surrender we are giving up the source of all pain— duality; the illusion that we are separate from God and everyone else. Through regular and sincere prayer, we are able to shed this illusion, this sense that *I am separate from God*, which is central to the ego.

There are many people who demand something of God during prayer. This is not praying. A demanding mind-set is simply our mind and ego wanting to do business with God. You cannot pray with an arrogant mind; deep prayer comes out of humility.

We must learn to surrender our mind and ego during prayer; there should be no sense of "I" or "me" during true worship or meditation. When we truly surrender our heart to silent prayer and God, what we are communicating is T*hy will be done.* What this means is that I, as an ego/personality, am willing to obey my Higher Self, my inner God in all life situations. In this sense, we accept a spirit of servitude during prayer.

Think of God as your own mother or father. God flows in every one of our veins. You do not have to pray in a formal manner; just ask God for something the way a child lovingly asks his mother— *mamma, please give me this.*

Sometimes God places us in very difficult situations. Through sincere prayer and ego-surrender, we communicate our intent and willingness to wait patiently until God reveals the real meaning or truth of a situation. Deep, sincere prayer offered in total surrender and humility helps us stay calm in difficult situations until God reveals the underlying reason why we are facing that situation. Once we understand the revelation of God, the simplicity of Her answer is astounding.

From Prayer Arises the Voice of Our Heart

During solitary prayer, we hear our own deepest voice. Anytime we make contact with our own deepest voice, our essence, we shed layers of our false Self (ego) and realize our truest Self (Soul). Regular prayer sessions conducted in a spirit of honesty, will in turn, make one very honest with oneself.

The voice of our Self which arises from our silent depths is also the voice of our heart. Prayer opens our heart and thus serves to deepen our meditation. An open heart is one place we can always feel the presence of God.

Understand that true meditation is not about mastering techniques; deep meditation comes from an open, devoted, and loving heart seeking our truest essence. Regular prayer sessions serve to keep our heart open and our emotions flowing. In this sense, prayer is a tool for spiritual and emotional maintenance.

Prayer Benefits Our Physical Wellbeing

Prayer also benefits our physical wellbeing. Just as silver needs periodic polishing, we need to polish our heart through regular prayer. When our heart is closed and our emotions blocked, we hinder the movement of the Life Force that flows through all 72,000 of our energy centers (*nadis*). Blocking the flow of the Life Force impacts our health and sense of wellbeing. As discussed in Lesson 16 (Human *Chakras*), the health and balance of our Life Force is much more important than later curing illness in the physical body. Hence, prayer is critical to our health and wellbeing.

Factors that Stengthen Our Prayer

The power of our prayers depends on three factors:

1. The strength of emotions behind our prayers: When we *emotionalize* our prayer, those thoughts have greater power to deeply penetrate space.

2. Faith: Our prayers are answered only when we truly believe the God Force will answer our prayers. Prayer without absolute certainty that the God Force will hear and answer you is not effective.

3. Concentration and focus of the mind: When we pray deeply, our mind becomes very single-pointed and focused on the God Force and the subject of our prayer. Random thoughts arising from mind chatter dissipate within a few inches of our body and never penetrate very far. However, when we clear our rambling mind of random thoughts and focus our thought-waves deeply on one topic, like a laser beam, we produce very high frequency thought-waves that penetrate space for vast distances.

The Role of Faith

Our powerful intentions actually stir and influence the quantum God Force. Our intentions and thoughts are only powerful when we believe and have faith in these notions.

Here, I would like you to understand a simple truth about prayer—*your prayers will only be answered if you believe that God will answer your prayers.* If you pray for something with your entire heart and Being, that prayer will surely be answered. Most people pray as a last resort; they are already hopeless before beginning the prayer session. This kind of prayer has no power.

Distant Prayer Groups (*Yagya*)

There are times when a group of people come together to pray for a common cause. Such group prayer sessions are most powerful when the prayer is directed at a subject other than one's own self. In India, distant prayer for a cause or a person outside the prayer group is called *yagya*. In the West, it has been proven in dozens of medical studies that distant prayer groups praying for the recovery of a sick person can drastically accelerate healing and improvement in the health of that patient.

The Three Steps of Prayer

Most people do not realize that prayer is a three step process:

1. Asking for guidance or results

2. Hearing God's response

3. Being open to receiving God's grace

The first step of prayer is probably the easiest, as most of us are comfortable asking for guidance or results. What is more challenging is steps two and three which are essential components of prayer that are often overlooked. There are many people who pray, but do not realize that after prayer we have to listen deeply for God's answer. The person who prays sincerely and humbly activates the second step of prayer by then listening with their heart for God's answer. Always await God's answer within your heart. The third step of prayer requires us to remain open to receiving God's grace. We are most open to God's blessing when our heart is open, when we have faith, and when we believe in our own worthiness.

The Ways God Answers our Prayers

Our inner God usually responds to our prayers in a delicate manner. It is important we are open and receptive so that we can catch Her subtle message. The God Force will use one or more of the following methods to get our attention:

Inner-Voice

God's response sometimes comes to us in the form of words. However, we must listen carefully to discern between the voice of ego and the voice of God; the voice of God is very different from the voice of ego. The voice of ego is loud, stubborn, and has a selfish attitude of "What is in this for me?" There is always a selfish, fearful energy in the voice of ego.

The voice of God, on the other hand, is very subtle, loving and persistent. Our inner God does not leave us alone. We hear the same gentle, loving, simple, yet grand message time after time. It is our ego and mind that choose to ignore the voice of our inner God.

Dreams

Many dreams that contain God's message are symbolic. But dreams that contain God's answers to our prayers have a very different quality from sporadic, night time dreams. The divine dreams have a quality of crystal clarity, just like direct experience. The person having had such a dream often reports that the sensation and message of the dream stayed with them long after waking. These types of dreams leave a lasting impression.

Synchronistic Events

God's response to us sometimes comes in the form of synchronistic events. These are events such as a chance meeting with a person who provides an answer to our problem; turning to a page in a book that contains a special message; an unexpected change in your life situation; or going out into nature and receiving an answer from the stars, a river, an old tree, etc. Some people refer to synchronistic events as serendipity.

Intuitive Thoughts or Ideas

God's response to us sometimes comes in the form of intuitive thoughts or ideas that come in a sudden flash, seemingly out of nowhere. Often these thoughts or ideas are not something we consciously asked for.

Direct Communion and Dialogue with the God Force

Gradually, through continued prayer, meditation and receptive listening, we actually feel a direct communion and dialogue with the God Force. This is the highest form of bliss and the end of all fear and pain; we no longer *believe* in God but rather *know* that we are One with God and that God truly is omnipresent – everywhere evenly present, within and all around us.

Lesson 27

Self-Esteem

Self-esteem is our mental concept of who we are. I say *mental* because who we think we are is almost never accurate. Our mental concepts come from a mind conditioned by old thoughts and past experiences. We are spiritual Beings who are valuable regardless of what we do or achieve in life. We do not have to do anything to become valuable.

You are and always have been...

The Roots of Low Self-Esteem

During childhood, certain painful events occur that distort our idea of our own value and worthiness. This damaged and warped sense of who we are becomes the identity we carry with us through our teenage years and into adulthood. As we encounter other painful life-experiences along the way, we develop more layers of inner pain that further distorts our sense of self-esteem.

Here are some examples of events and factors that contribute to low self-esteem:

- Death of a parent

- Divorce of parents

- A parent or a spouse who is emotionally unavailable

- Parents, teachers, siblings or friends that constantly criticize us

- An illness or physical handicap that makes us feel inadequate or different from others

- A life event such as financial bankruptcy or political revolution that creates turmoil, confusion and deep emotional pain

- Any factor or life event that seems to validate our sense of unworthiness

It is important to understand that the actual event is really irrelevant to our self-esteem; it is always our interpretation of what really happened and what that event meant to us emotionally that later limits our spiritual growth.

Healing Our Inner Pain

As adults who have decided to heal, we need to make sense of what happened in our past that caused deep internal scars and lessened our self-esteem. We need to remember our interpretation of what happened and we need to change our perception of what really happened to a more positive one. We have to understand that our inner pain comes from our unhealthy perception of what really happened. Having changed our perception, we can now let go of pain that we have held inside for such a long time. For many of us, this is a daunting challenge and we succumb to fear driven complacency, we give in to our familiarity with the pain. Many times, our deep seated pain has become a part of us, like our right arm. Some people are so attached to their familiar pain it is as if they are married to the pain.

To look at all this positively, all of us must remember that we were strong enough to survive any physical, emotional, or spiritual hardship that we underwent during childhood. We are still here and alive because we are strong and because the God Force flows beneath every atom of our body.

If you are thinking about taking action or have already taken steps toward reconciling and letting go of your pain, use your faith and the strengths you had as a child to help guide you! The rest of this lesson will explore other insights and tools that will support your healing process.

Understanding Defense Mechanisms

Because feeling unworthy is too painful to feel, we protect ourselves against deep hurt through two types of defense mechanisms:

1. We block our emotions and bury our hurt deep in our subconscious and we build other defense mechanisms to protect ourselves against the pain.

2. To digest and justify the painful event that made us feel unworthy, we form a core belief that *I deserved what happened to me because I am unworthy as a human being—I am not okay.*

While defense mechanisms might seem to initially help us cope with inner pain, years later, after they become habitual, these old defenses block the flow of energy, creativity and vitality through our body. Defense mechanisms choke the movement of the Life Force through our energy channels (*nadis*).

Remember, the God Force and all of life created by God is made of fluid energy. When we defend ourselves against emotional energy we are literally blocking the flow of life through our body. To be a free liberated person, you must let all of life flow through you. A free person is a powerful person.

Symptoms of Low Self-Esteem

Anyone suffering from low self-esteem will identify with some of these symptoms. Think about the questions below, and answer them honestly. These questions come from a psychological questionnaire designed to gauge the level of people's self-esteem.

This questionnaire is beneficial in identifying unconscious mental habits that limit your growth. Please do not judge or belittle yourself if some of these conditions apply to you. Remember, you have the power of God within you; you can free yourself from any self-limiting habit.

Self-Esteem Checklist

- *Do I spend much time daydreaming and fantasizing?*

- *Have I spent long periods of my life in general depression, sadness and hopelessness?*

- *Do I remain in abusive relationships?*

- *Am I clear and certain about my decisions and my life direction?*

- *Do I often wish I was someone else with a different personality?*

- *Do I feel I am generally a likeable person?*

- *Do I get along well with my parents, brothers and sisters?*

- *Am I often worried about various aspects of my life?*

- *Is it difficult for me to speak in front of an audience?*

- *Do I often wish I was younger?*

- *Do I wish I could change and improve many aspects of myself?*

- *Can I make important life decisions easily?*

- *Do others enjoy their relationships with me?*

- *When at home, am I easily upset and disturbed by unexpected events?*

- *Do I complete all tasks well and completely?*

- *Am I proud of my educational and professional accomplishments?*

- *Is it more comfortable for someone else to guide me through life decisions?*

- *Am I uncomfortable and confused about change; do I take a long time to adjust to change?*

- *Do I often regret my decisions later?*

- *Do I have credibility amongst people my own age?*

- *Am I easily discouraged and defeated in challenging situations?*

- *Do I take good care of myself, physically and emotionally?*

- *Am I more comfortable associating and working with people of lower intelligence and capabilities?*

- *Do I feel as though my parents and spouse have unreasonable expectations of me?*

- *Did I enjoy the teacher calling on me for answers in the classroom when I was a young student?*

- *Do I know myself and the desires of my heart well?*

- *Do I often create unnecessary problems, turmoil and trouble in my inner life?*

- *Do I feel like my life has been very difficult and full of pain?*

- *Do I feel like my parents, spouse and children do not pay enough attention to me at home?*

- *Can I make a decision and stick to my decision no matter how great the challenge?*

- *Do I feel as though I cannot manage my daily responsibilities well enough?*

- *Am I ignorant of my strengths, beauty, accomplishments and positive aspects?*

- *Do I enjoy socializing or do I resist social situations?*

- *Am I afraid to be at home alone? Am I easily bored with myself?*

- *Do I often feel guilty or carry a sense of shame about myself?*

- *Do I feel stuck and helpless during challenging situations?*

- *Am I less optimistic than other people around me?*

- *If I feel a strong emotion or when I have a personal need, can I express it to others easily and honestly?*

- *Do I feel like the people close to me are often critical of me?*

- *Do I become defensive when someone else's opinion differs from mine?*

- *Do I feel close to my family? Do my family members really understand me?*

- *Do I value life or do I not really care how long I remain alive?*

- *Do I feel like life has defeated me?*

- *Am I easily and deeply hurt when others criticize me?*

- *Am I always looking up to others and respecting others more than I respect myself?*

- *Do I feel like my family members are always putting me under a lot of pressure?*

- *Do I easily express my inner truth, emotions and needs to others?*

- *Am I easily agitated and irritated?*

- *Do I have great difficulty getting involved in relationships? Can I trust and feel close to others?*

Emotional Effects of Low Self-Esteem

Whether or not you were able to identify with some of the characteristics of low self-esteem mentioned in the checklist above, you may recognize some of the symptoms of low self-esteem. Below are some of the emotional effects of low self-esteem:

Depression

Continuous feelings of unworthiness cause depression. We are all spiritual Beings with the God Force flowing beneath every atom of our body. In other words, we are gods. When we belittle ourselves, we are insulting God and our own Soul. This causes depression.

We also feel depressed when we turn our anger and frustration inwards. This happens when we are afraid to express our needs and protect our personal boundaries.

Inner-shame

Beliefs about our own unworthiness also create a feeling of inner shame. We are ashamed of who we are because somehow we feel like we are not okay. We believe that if we were to reveal our truest self to someone else, they would no longer value us as the person we really are.

Guilt

Low self-esteem also creates guilt. When we do not believe in ourselves, we often feel guilty about what we think, do and say. We blame ourselves for everything and even feel guilty about other peoples' emotions.

Feeling Our Real Emotions

When we defend ourselves against pain and bury our hurt deep in our subconscious, we shut down emotionally. Some people cling to old wounds, self-pity, and revenge toward those who hurt them in the past. Holding on to these old emotions is inappropriate in the present moment. This attitude really hurts our Soul. Clinging to old pain makes us apathetic toward life, causing the love and joy in our heart to dry up and making us bitter people.

It takes a lot of courage to relive and feel our hidden emotions and pain again. We must go beyond the limits of our fears, uncover and reconnect with our hidden emotions. Those who walk through these dark clouds will find insight and happiness on the other side of the emotional storm. When you walk through your fire without fear and with lots of faith, you will find lasting contentment on the other side.

When we uncover and feel our powerful emotions, we release tremendous energy that was previously blocked in our body. During the process of healing we forgive those who hurt us, not for the sake of those other people, but for the sake of our own physical, emotional, and spiritual wellbeing.

Exercise – Letting Go

Understand that it feels very threatening to uncover old wounds. You can carry this simple technique with you and practice it as often as necessary. It will allow you to maintain awareness, altitude and liberation as you experience powerful emotions.

As you make contact with old emotions, stay with your breath. With each exhalation, say in your mind "let go, let go". As you exhale, relax your grip on old wounds, release your unhealthy perceptions with each exhalation. With each exhalation, relax your mind and every muscle of your body and let the negativity flow out of your nostrils.

Understanding Addictions

Addictions reflect a sense of low self-esteem. All addictions are a substitute for lack of an inner life and self-love. When we have no relationship with the Self, we feel an inner vacuum that we must fill with an external distraction such as drugs, alcohol, pornography, TV, video games, endless partying, etc. The addictive substance or activity subconsciously fills a hole, it fills a type of inner emptiness that comes from inner pain. Addictions always serve to numb our inner pain.

Instead of facing and feeling our wound with awareness, we cover it up with an addiction. In order not to feel our emotions, we overindulge in food, sex, movies, drugs or dinner parties. Some people create such a busy work schedule that they do not have time to feel their emotions.

We must understand that there can be no substitute for an inner life and for self-love. We must make contact with our inner God and listen to God's voice within our heart.

The Inner Child

Inside each person, there lives a little child who controls our most primal, authentic and powerful emotions. All of our deepest fears, insecurities and anger are reflections of this inner child. Conversely, our creativity, joy and spontaneity also arise from this inner child.

In order to release past hurt that we are holding inside, we must reacquaint ourselves with this child and promise to love him unconditionally. Pray to your inner child, ask for her help; ask what she needs. Ask yourself, *what are the most important priorities in my life?* The answers will come from your inner child, speaking through your heart. Paying attention to your inner child is the same as taking care of your deepest needs.

Overcoming Low Self-Esteem

The most sacred relationship is with your Self (Soul). Understand that if we do not love ourselves we cannot love anyone else. It is impossible to develop and maintain a healthy relationship if we do not love ourselves. We must develop an inner life and take care of our deepest needs.

When we begin to love and care deeply for our self, feelings of unworthiness slowly fade. The best way to eliminate low self-esteem is to love ourselves deeply.

Here are some suggestions for taking better care of your Soul in order to raise your self-esteem:

- **Take time every day for quiet meditation**. Witness your passing thoughts and emotions with relaxed awareness. Observe the old stories and messages going through your mind.

- **Pray every day**. When you pray, pray with a sincere heart, not from your ego and mind. Prayer is a way of connecting with the truth of your heart. After your daily prayers, listen for God's answer to each prayer. Stay open and very quiet in order to hear God's answer to your prayer.

- **Make it a daily practice to do three loving things for yourself**. Examples are good food, a bath, a nice walk, exercise, etc.

- **Listen to beautiful music, dance, or sing everyday**. Listen deeply to every note and let the musical vibrations pass through your body. Feel the notes in your heart. Feel the movements in your body tissue.

- **Surround yourself with unconditionally loving people**. These kinds of relations are hard to find, but if you commit to self-love and ask for loving people, they will appear in your life. Call people you really love, go and visit them.

- **Feel your authentic emotions**. If you feel anxiety or pain inside, let that discomfort flow through you. Do not block it or run away from it through addictions. Just be with your emotion while you maintain full awareness through breath and body consciousness.

- **Express your creativity**. Your creativity comes from your Soul, from your inner child. Partake in your favorite creative act—dance, paint, sing, write poetry, etc. The creative act that is most natural to you will arouse deep feelings of love in your heart. If there is a form of creativity that brings tears to your eyes, pay attention to it because that is where the spiritual treasure lies.

- **Go out and be with nature**. Listen to all the sounds, see all the colors, smell all the scents. Once your mind quiets, ask God, *are You here with me?* Listen deeply for God's presence all around you.

- **Put yourself in the service of others**. Serving others will deflate your wounded ego. Give unconditional love to others, you will see that you receive tenfold for all that you give to others. When you experience this spiritual truth, you will trust life and other people much more.

- **Treat yourself to a body massage**. We hold a lot of pain in our body. Body massages given by the right person are very healing.

Lesson 28

Affirmations

The subconscious mind, which controls about 70 percent of our daily behavior, actualizes and materializes any thought that we feed it. Affirmations are statements (intentional thoughts), made in the present tense, that we feed the subconscious mind in order to reprogram and replace previous negative self-talk.

So, affirmations are seed thoughts that we plant in our subconscious mind. Once we plant seeds of positive thinking in our mind, these seeds grow like a tree. They develop branches and soon enough we witness dramatic changes in our core beliefs, energy, behavior, and overall life.

Understanding Negative Thought Patterns

In our past, certain events occurred which we interpreted as being our fault or some negative reflection of who we are. You might recall in the 'cycle of illusion' introduced in Lesson 15 (The Mind) that our personal interpretation of what really happened differs from the utter reality of what happened. In other words, the actual event is different from our perception of the event. It is our perception that we interpret as real and internalize as a reflection of who we are. When our perception of an event is negative, we often view ourself negatively.

Once we have formed that core belief that somehow we are not okay, negative messages (self-talk) start playing in our subconscious mind over and over again, like a cassette tape. Any message repeated in the mind turns into a belief and beliefs begin influencing our behavior which then creates our life's results.

Replacing Negative Self-Talk

We have the choice to replace negative self-talk with positive affirmations. After all, negativity and destructive thoughts are simply mental habits that we have grown accustomed to. Most of us have become so accustomed to these habits we would go to any length to defend our beliefs.

Positive affirmations have a powerful effect on changing self-limiting beliefs lodged in our subconscious mind. To maximize the power of positive seed thoughts, we can repeat our chosen affirmation(s) 100 to 400 times a day. You might recite your affirmation in your mind, in front of the mirror, or even sing your affirmation out loud.

How to Create Affirmations Suited to Your Needs

Each person's affirmations are unique because each one of us is a unique creation of God; we each have different needs and different negative mental habits. Your affirmations should neutralize your negative self-concepts and transform these self-destructive beliefs into confidence and joy. Affirmative statements should always be in the present tense. If you state your affirmations in the past or future tenses, the God Force will not deliver what you need right now.

Ask yourself the following questions. If you have negative answers to these questions, you can compose positive affirmations that counter your negativities in these areas of life:

- What do I believe about Life?

- *What do I believe about my Self* (spiritually, emotionally, physically, socially and financially)?

- What do I believe about God?

- What do I want most in my life? Do I believe I can get it?

Never affirm what you do not want in your life. Negative affirmations create exactly what we do not want in life. You will recall from previous lessons that the subconscious mind responds to all our thoughts; if we constantly obsess about what we do not want to happen, the subconscious will take those same dreaded elements and manifest them in our life. Remember, the subconscious mind and the God Force are mirrors that reflect the reality of what is in your mind back to you!

Examples of Positive Affirmations

Remember, it is important to formulate positive affirmations in the present tense. Affirmations stated in past or future tense confuse the God Force making it impossible for Her to deliver what you need in the present. Below are a few examples of positive affirmations in the present tense:

> *My heart is filled with love.*

> *I am a child of God.*

> *The light of God shines within me.*

> *I love and approve of myself.*

> *I am eternally energetic and young.*

My life is full of love, joy and wealth.

Abundance, wealth and comfort are now flowing into my life.

There are dozens of people who love me deeply.

My inner wisdom has answers to all my questions.

The Reaction of Your Body and Mind to Affirmations

As you practice positive affirmations, pay attention to the reaction of your mind and body as you repeat your affirmations. At first, your mind and ego will make fun of the affirmation exercise. The mind will throw in comments and negativities like, *this is so stupid, I am never going to have these good things by just repeating these sentences!*

You may also find that your muscles become tense as you repeat positive affirmations about your life. Do not give any energy to your internal resistance, breathe into your body and continue to repeat your positive affirmations.

As you pick up on the different sensations reciting positive affirmations bring to your mind and body, continue to be loving and gentle with yourself. Do not get frustrated at any perceived resistance. Absorbing affirmations into our subconscious takes time; it also takes commitment and love.

Lesson 29

Developing the Courage to Change

In order to transform and improve our outer life, we must begin with the healing and transformation of our inner life. The spiritual life lies within, not on the outside. Those who achieve personal growth make a vow to their Soul to persistently work on themselves from inside out and to apply spiritual principles and the laws of nature to their day-to-day lives.

Focus On Yourself

Many of us have felt at some time or another that we can change a loved one. It is true that each of us is an agent of transformation. However, what most of us neglect to realize is that in order to help transform others, we must first transform ourselves.

To love others, we must first love ourselves. To be able to serve others, we must absolutely and always serve our own Soul (Higher Self). The most powerful way to inspire others is to reach your own dreams and perfection. Keep reminding yourself:

Everything is created from inside out.

The spiritual warrior is constantly studying her own mind, thoughts and actions in order to dive deeper and understand the Self (Soul). To accomplish anything, we must first develop our character, courage, and a healthy mind and nervous system.

Exercise – Identifying Core Beliefs and Values

Study yourself everyday by observing your mind and emotions like a witness. Every time you lose contact with the Witness, follow the movement of your inhalation and exhalation with keen awareness and again begin observing your mind and emotions. Notice the recurring thoughts; what are your core beliefs and values that underlie your recurring thoughts? Which sorts of top priorities seem to underlie your goals and desires? Which thoughts and fantasies really energize you?

Releasing Our Resistance to Change

The God Force is subatomic energy that is fluid and constantly reshaping itself into millions of different forms. All of nature is constantly changing and evolving every second. We, as humans who are God's creation, must also change and evolve everyday in order to be in harmony with the laws of nature. When we resist change, we are sabotaging the process of self-transformation. When we resist the changes that this moment brings, we experience stress. Be fluid, like water; embrace and relax into the moment. By doing so, you will find the most appropriate, least resistant path.

The remainder of this lesson will explore different aspects of growth that will help you develop the courage to change and support you on your journey.

Understand the Way the Mind and Ego Resists Change

Those parts of us that resist change are the mind and ego. Ego and mind cling to what is familiar and strongly resist stepping into the unknown. Since the spiritual world and your inner life are a mystery, they are a world unknown to your mind and ego and therefore quite threatening.

Through meditation, spiritual study, and other spiritual practices, we train the mind and ego to feel more comfortable with stepping into the unknown.

Understand Fear

Fear is the source of all personal resistance; fear stops us from following our dreams. Think about all the ways that you have wanted to grow and how you sabotaged that transformation process. In your final analysis, you discover that the force blocking all personal change and growth is fear.

Exercise—Dispelling Fear

To review, fear is not something real; fear is something we unconsciously manufacture as a product of the mind.

> The instant you sense fear arise in your mind, brush it away by thinking the opposite, positive and constructive thought. The way to de-energize thoughts is to purposely place your attention on another thought. This practice takes energy away from fearful impulses and prevents fears from multiplying and draining your Life Force. Another strategy to block fear from taking root in your mind is to take full deep breaths into your stomach whenever you sense an attack of fear. This type of breathing immediately affects your physiology by changing the chemistry of your blood from acid to base. Slow, deep belly-breathing, with concentration on the inhalation and exhalation, brings you to the present moment, and empties your mind of fearful and distracting thoughts. Let each exhalation be a wave that washes away all thoughts. Allow each exhalation to wash away your fearful thoughts right out of your nostrils.

Exercise - Directly Challenging Fear

Another very powerful practice is to purposely do all the things that you fear most while vigilantly following your inhalation and exhalation. When you put yourself in a fearful situation and are willing to directly face your fears, you witness your fears vanishing like a mirage in the desert. Know that all your fears will vanish the instant you face them and look them straight in the eyes while maintaining breath awareness.

Know Your Self

Spiritual growth requires that we go deeper and deeper in order to know our self. Meditate daily and observe your thoughts and emotions from a higher elevation, without being entangled with passing thoughts and emotions. When you witness passing thoughts and emotions you are separate from thoughts yet can still feel your emotions as a detached Witness. Each time you meditate, you dive deeper into emptiness. Make it the intention of your spiritual practice to know yourself spiritually, emotionally, mentally and physically.

Knowing the Self is not an intellectual effort, you do not have to strain your mind. Just the opposite, ride the motion of your breath or a *mantra* during meditation and let the busy mind vanish into nothingness. In that vast, empty space, you will meet your most authentic self.

Develop Emotional Intelligence

Emotional intelligence means knowing what you are thinking, the emotions you are feeling, and your physical sensations at any given moment. Maintain awareness on the inner physical sensations of your body. Through this constant practice, you will come to know your inner world intimately. You will know what intuitively feels right or when you are on the wrong path.

Know Your Mission (Calling)

Once you get to know yourself, you will understand your life purpose. Your life purpose is your mission to God and also your passion. You were born for that purpose in this lifetime. Your life purpose is your promise to your inner God; how to serve your inner God and society through your most natural, God-given talents.

When you understand your reason for being in this life, you will know what your most important life priorities are. When you understand what your life is all about, you will wake up each morning with energy, joy and a sense of direction.

Focus on Your Life Purpose; Avoid Distractions

Having identified your highest life priorities, follow the important spiritual practice of throwing away all useless distractions that take you away from your life priorities. Time is invaluable; we only have so much of it in each lifetime, and once lost, we never retrieve lost moments of opportunity. Develop personal discipline to minimize distractions. Develop the discipline of avoiding procrastination. Learn to say "no" to any activity that distracts you from your main mission. Work steadily everyday to fulfill your life purpose. Whatever your life passion may be, serve others as you follow your own calling.

Determine Your Goals

Your destiny has to do with the overall direction and purpose of your life. To carry out your mission, you need to translate your broader vision into smaller more detailed goals and steps. These goals represent steps that you need to take to reach your final destination.

Take a few minutes each month to write down your goals. When you set and write down goals for yourself, you send a message to your subconscious mind to organize all necessary resources to achieve your goals. Goal-setting automatically triggers your mind and the Life Force to mobilize all resources in the necessary direction. It is important to write down your goals as your subconscious responds more definitively towards goals that are written down.

Utilize Creative Visualization

The subconscious mind understands images much better than verbal orders. When you come to know who you are and set your goals, spend 5 minutes three times a day visualizing the desirable outcomes of your life, exactly the way your heart wants them. Visualize the life that fulfills you by engaging your five senses in the visualization. During your visualization exercise, go into full detail; imagine everything, every step leading to the life you truly want. Visualize the greatest that you can be; even visualize your own joy at living the life you wish to live. It is important to *emotionalize* your visualizations.

Creative visualization gives us a clear vision of the outcome of our life's work. Visualization exercises program our subconscious mind to believe what we are visualizing. Remember, the subconscious mind does not differentiate between your present reality and the one that you are visualizing for your future. Once your subconscious mind truly believes in the possibility of an alternative reality, the subconscious mind acts like a powerful magnet to attract exactly those circumstances that correspond to your new beliefs.

Incorporate Daily Reading as a Spiritual Practice

Expanding our knowledge is an important part of daily spiritual practice. Take some time during your day or right before sleep to read. Imagine, if you read 15 minutes a day you will finish several books a year!

Choose reading material that is uplifting to your spirit and mind. Be very selective about what you read. Classic scriptures, spiritual books and autobiographies of inspiring people will give you powerful energy.

Do not just read books. Studying inspiring books without applying their truth to your daily life makes spiritual reading just another burdensome chore. When you read this material, do not skim over or skip pages. Read slowly and absorb the information in your heart. Contemplate the truth of what you are reading. Take time to sit with the material and sense whether it rings true in your heart.

Reading positive and uplifting material just before sleep is especially beneficial because whatever enters your mind right before deep sleep programs and trains your subconscious mind. When you wake up the next morning, that inspiring information will have deeply penetrated your subconscious mind during the restful hours of the night.

Take Time for Daily Contemplation

Late in the evening, before you sleep, take time to contemplate that day's thoughts, emotions, actions and activities that you were engaged in.

Which thoughts, emotions, actions, or activities made you a better person? Which contributed to you being the greatest person you can be? Which thoughts, emotions, actions, or activities belittled your Soul? I believe that God is very happy with us when we love ourselves deeply. If you imagine that God was holding your hand during the entire day, what part of your day would make God smile?

At the end of your silent contemplation period, make a vow to yourself that you will only give energy to those elements that deepen your self-love (not egotistical selfishness), and enhance your personal growth.

Apply the Rule of 21 Days

Research shows that it takes the subconscious mind 21 days of practice to adopt a new habit. If you stay focused on your personal goals and any positive new habit for 21 days, that new habit will become part of your natural personality.

As you develop the courage to change, set goals and institute new spiritual practices, honor the rule of 21 days and see how effortless long-term change becomes. You will experience how easy it is to reap the rewards of commitment.

Exercise – Clearly Defining Your Goals

When you set personal goals, be sure to attach a deadline to each goal. Defining a timeframe for each goal energizes that goal and commits the mind and Spirit to achieving that goal within the specified timeframe.

You can define goals for all areas of your life:

- Spiritual

- Financial

- Professional (work or study-related)

- Emotional

- Physical

- Social/Family-Related

- Spiritual

Examples of spiritual goals might include getting up earlier in the morning, doing Yoga exercises, eating fresh fruit and vegetables, meditating, studying spiritual literature and developing a clear mind and a calm nervous system.

The minute you set your goals and commit to their achievement, all natural forces within and outside of you unite to support you in your cause. Your life will be transformed the instant you truly commit to goals.

Goal-setting is a means of focusing your personal attention on something. Remember this spiritual law:

Whatever you put your attention on will grow.

Lesson 30

Developing a Mind of Unlimited Potential

In Lesson 15 (The Mind), we learned that our mind is our most powerful instrument. The human mind is a powerful magnet that attracts anything we mentally focus on. You see, everything in this world is created twice – once in our mind, and then, as material reality. Our thoughts are bundles of subatomic energy that go out like messengers and summon the very circumstances that you are mentally concentrating on. Ponder this truth:

You achieve whatever you conceive!

Dare to Realize the Unlimited Potential of Your Mind

The advanced Yogis of India and the Dervishes of Persia have exemplified the unlimited potential of our mind. They can actually stop their heart and perform many other miraculous feats by simply focusing their minds on that act.

The majority of people in this world are only using ten percent of their mental potential, a miniscule fraction of what our mind is capable of! Imagine developing a mind of unlimited potential like the advanced Yogis of India and the Dervishes of Persia. The Yogis and Dervishes remind us that we must never underestimate the power of our mind.

The remainder of this lesson will explore ways you can work on developing a mind of unlimited potential.

Be Conscious of What You Feed Your Mind

Many people think that their mind is an autonomous, independent entity with its own power of manipulation over its owner. This is an illusion; your mind is merely a mirror, it simply reflects your own input back to you. Ultimately, you have control about what you put into your mind.

What I am hinting at is that God has given you free will, the power of choice over what you put into your mind. So, be very careful what you feed your mind. Be selective about the people you associate with, the movies you see, the magazines/newspapers you read, the conversations you listen to, the Internet sites you visit, etc. Only allow the best nourishment to enter your mind.

Resist Worry

One element that drains away all of our *Prana* and destroys the mind's vitality is worry. The untrained mind is always drowning in worrisome thoughts which are either about the past or the future, never about this moment. Thinking about the past or the future always creates worry and anxiety in our mind, and worry is like a disease that quickly manifests a whirlwind of symptoms.

Worry also tires the mind. As powerful as your mind is, if that same mind is tired, restless, or agitated you will not be able to accomplish anything. An agitated and distracted mind will consume all of the Life Force (*Prana*) in your body.

As you strive to develop a mind of unlimited potential, resist the temptation of worry as worry only serves to limit the expanse of your mind and have negative effects on you physically, emotionally, mentally and spiritually.

Choose Your Thoughts

At the first appearance of a negative thought-wave, replace that negative impulse of energy with a positive energizing thought. If you do not catch the destructive thought at the onset, a few moments later that wave of negativity will have multiplied and you will face a storm.

Exercise - Witnessing Thoughts

The first step in healing your mind is to simply observe the mind and notice what kinds of thoughts you are having. Make this a daily spiritual practice; develop your capacity to stand aside and witness your passing thoughts and emotions.

Sitting alone in a private place, place your fingers in both ears, then, witness your own thoughts and emotions. As you observe them, whisper the message of each passing thought as if an announcer is announcing the arrival of each thought on the screen of the mind. Become the sportscaster who is announcing the players (thoughts) entering the stadium (mind). During this entire exercise simply remain the observer, like a sportscaster. As soon as you are pulled into the thought, step out by following your inhalation and exhalation for a moment. Then, go back and continue announcing the arrival of each thought in a whisper. Hear your own whisper announcing each new thought and emotion entering the stadium field of the mind.

Understand the Role of *Samskaras*

The average human mind thinks sixty thousand thoughts per day. Out of that many thoughts, 95 percent are repetitive thoughts that you have been circulating in your mind every day for years. Most of these repetitive thoughts are of no use since they are not related to the needs of this moment.

It is the habit of the conditioned mind to swim in circles, to get stuck in its old repetitive patterns. In the Sanskrit language, these repetitious and unconscious mental habits are called *samskaras*.

Destructive, negative thoughts that continue to play in your mind like a cassette tape are only mental habits. Do not confuse these with the real you. They have power over you only when you are unaware of them. As soon as you step back and witness your thoughts and emotions they lose their grip over you.

Exercise—Replacing Bad Habits

The nature of the mind is to become addicted to habits. Although it is not possible to eliminate habits, we can replace a bad habit with a good one in 21 days.

Gather your courage and practice replacing negative thoughts and habits with empowering ones for 21 days in a row. For example, you can practice waking earlier, walking 25 percent faster, eating a vegetarian diet, exercising and doing Yoga, or affirming positive aspects of yourself. Whatever new thought or habit you introduce, commit to following through with it for 21 days. After that period of time all of these practices will have become second nature.

Take Control of Your Mind

Healing your mind and achieving spiritual progress require dedicated effort. The spiritual odyssey is not for the coward or impatient person. While most people have no idea of the immensity of their spiritual potential, our inner God demands that we remain spiritual warriors under all circumstances.

The spiritual life is a full-time commitment. We cannot live a spiritual life 50 percent of the time. This is just the mind and ego fooling us into thinking that we can fool our own inner God.

Every hour of every day, dedicate all your energy to healing your inner life, mastering your mind, and staying in contact with your Soul (inner God). Always remember it is never any external event that disturbs our peace; it is always our mental reaction to an event that determines how we experience that situation.

Never give up and do not be disheartened by daily fluctuations in your consciousness. After all, human consciousness is subatomic energy that is fluid and constantly in flux. You must make your spiritual practice a steady, continuous, and long-term practice. With this kind of strategy you will see how much more clarity and inner peace you achieve every six months!

Search for the Positive in Life

Always search for the positive element in every person and in each circumstance of your life. Believe me, each of us can find at least one positive element in any situation.

An important point to understand is that there are no mistakes, only life lessons to be learned. If your truest intention is developing wisdom, self-mastery and self-transformation, then you will wake up each day with the attitude: *today I will live in the present moment, fully awake and aware of the lessons that this day will bring.*

Live Your Dreams Passionately

When we are children, we live spontaneously in the moment. Each moment we follow our joys, our sense of playfulness. The pleasures of children are simple; children can find magic in the simplest of situations. They are natural adventurers who are curious and passionate about discovering the unknown.

You too were once a child and you still have a child living inside your heart.

As we grow up, during the education and socialization process, other people and institutions burden our mind with their rules, codes of conduct and their notion of reality. Although intuitively these guidelines may not make sense to us, as children, at some point in our lives, most of us abandon our hopes and dreams to fit the regulations set by society.

To be truly joyful again, we must open our hearts. The heart can only be open when we dare to follow our dreams. Each time someone else forces their reality into your mind you lose some degree of mental autonomy, spontaneity and passion. Ultimately, you should not pay any attention to other people's opinions and advice. It is not that they have bad intentions for you, but each person experiences life through their own limited mind and can only pass on their personal perspective to you.

To heal yourself, and make spiritual progress, you must strive toward the unlimited potential of your mind; you must follow your own dreams once again. Find out what it is that you are passionate about and then spend all your days following your truest passion with immense courage.

Techniques to Unleash Your Infinite Potential

Here are spiritual exercises that will unleash the infinite potential of your mind. Do these practices for 21 days and witness their powerful effect in your life.

Meditation

Meditate twice a day for 20 minutes per session. Let your mind sway with the movement of breath and let each exhalation relax your muscles. Allow each exhalation to wash away your thoughts, through your nostrils. Just 'be' in that vast sea of emptiness. You will come to know yourself well in that vast silent space.

Deep Breathing

Only breathe into your stomach, not your chest. Throughout the day, exercise slow, deep, rhythmic, and smooth belly breathing. When your mind is agitated, close your eyes and take 15 deep breaths into your stomach. When you slow down your breathing, the scattered mind becomes more calm and focused.

Replace Negative Thoughts with Positive Thoughts

Your passing thoughts and emotions are simply impulses of energy. Your mind can only think one thought at a time, so why occupy your precious mind with a negative notion. At the first sign of a negative thought, replace the negative thought-bubble with a positive one. Do not wait too long; if you allow negative thoughts to flourish, you will have a very tough struggle uprooting them.

Creative Visualization

Find out what it is that you want out of life; what makes you passionate and joyful? Each day, sit for 5 minutes before falling asleep and 5 minutes after you wake and visualize in full detail the desirable life situation that you want. Your subconscious mind is a powerful magnet that will create your desired situation for you.

Affirmations

Remember that your mind is only a mirror that reflects whatever you feed it. Create some positive, powerful affirmations such as:

I love myself deeply.
My life is full of love, joy and wealth.
Every answer that I need will come to me.

Repeat these affirmations 100-400 times daily as you go about your worldly responsibilities.

If you repeat and feel any affirmation for 21 days, your mind will permanently shift into that reality. When your mind adopts a belief, your new belief will change your behavior and automatically manifest the desired outcome for you.

Follow Your Intuition

Trust your own intuition. Listen to others but always test their advice to see if it rings true in your heart. No one knows you as well as yourself. Every day, practice following your own intuition even if others do not approve of your life direction.

Surrender

As you explore and utilize different spiritual practices, constantly surrender the practice and its outcome to the God Force. Ego and mind want to take credit for our spiritual growth, but ultimately it is the unlimited potential within us, our inner God, who blesses us with enlightenment.

Lesson 31

Compassion

Human beings, being social animals, need to interact and exchange love and compassion with one another. In the absence of love and compassion humans become deeply depressed. In essence, love is the nourishment that feeds the soul.

It has been shown that a baby nourished with food and drink but deprived of love and cuddling will develop intense emotional disorders, and the baby can actually die from lack of love. When the foetus is in its mother's womb, the mother's emotions affect the wellbeing of the baby. Most of our sense of security and trust in the flow of life develops between birth and the age of 3 to 5 years.

As grown-ups, our egotism, our sense of "I-ness", is an illusion that separates us from fellow human beings. In this illusion of separation we develop depression and the feeling of loneliness. Psychological research shows that the primary source of most mental illness is the lack of sympathy and connectedness with our fellow human beings and with our natural surroundings.

During deep states of meditation, our individual ego expands outward toward the all pervasive Soul and we become soul centered. Whenever we make contact with our soul we realize that there is only One Soul; we realize we are all One. For example, you may walk into a crowded street and feel like you know everyone intimately. With this sense of deep interconnection you internally grasp, with clarity, the sense that we all have the same desires – to be happy, pain free, and loved. When you realize our Oneness, that is compassion at its peak.

Compassion Arises From the Heart

Compassion arises from deep within our heart. Compassion is based on love and respect. Compassion also involves a deep sense of responsibility toward fellow human beings. A compassionate person cannot walk away knowing that another person is suffering. For example, if you witness a disastrous traffic accident and you drive away, your Life Force (*Prana)* will quickly diminish. This is because the injured soul that you are leaving behind is the same as your own.

Compassion is not the same as pity; when we pity someone, we are sending that person belittling and disempowering energy. Pity arises out of ego, not the heart and soul.

Some students think that you need to believe in God in order to be compassionate. Faith in God is not a prerequisite, and yet when we exercise deep compassion we come to feel God's presence in our heart and in everyone.

How Compassion Benefits Us

The wise person knows that love and compassion for all is actually a selfish act. This is because deep, sincere compassion wins you lasting friendships and unconditional love. When the time comes that you are truly in need, there will be many who are wholeheartedly willing to lend you a helping hand.

Compassion for others also puts our mind at ease. When we serve others with unconditional love, our heart opens, and a deep sense of peace and quietude overtakes us. In such a state the mind is clear.

Peace of mind nourishes the body since there is a close connection between a calm mind and physical wellbeing.

Developing compassion not only benefits our self, but has the potential to benefit a large populous. Compassion can have a ripple effect on a family, community or nation. When thousands of people develop and exercise compassion, an entire society behaves more responsibly. An entire country can run smoothly and efficiently when its people are compassionate.

The Great Obstacles to Compassion - Fear and Anger

The two forces that reduce our sense of compassion are fear and anger. Both of these emotions constrict our soul, our natural sense of greatness. As we learned in previous lessons, fear has a debilitating effect which impacts us mentally, emotionally, physically and spiritually. Thus, just like fear, anger has a profound impact on our overall wellbeing and effectively inhibits our natural compassion.

It is true that anger can be a source of energy. However, energy arising out of anger lacks a predictable direction. At times you may be able to direct your anger in a constructive manner, but because of its unpredictability, anger can just as well destroy you if it runs wild. Anger has the potential to swell until it dominates your entire mind. When you watch a raging person, you can see that this person has lost his mind. At the peak of anger, we can even become "mad with anger."

When someone approaches you with hatred and anger, remember breath awareness – *breath comes in, breath goes out.* While keeping a clear, calm mind, examine the other person and the reality of that particular situation. Perceive the whole circumstance as clearly as you are able, in the present moment. Your *sixth chakra*, the Third Eye, between the eyebrows, can help you perceive the underlying reality more clearly. When you understand the other person and that particular situation, you can minimize the energy of anger and take counter measures appropriate to that particular situation.

For example, imagine someone cuts in front of you in traffic and anger swells in your head. Before you react to the other driver, take three deep breaths and shift your consciousness into your heart area. When you do these two things, your reaction will arise out of compassion and understanding, not blind anger. In this example, you may instantly know that the other driver is under a lot of stress, causing that driver to drive without caution.

Remember that anger arises more frequently amongst people of lower consciousness. Individuals whose mind cannot reason clearly easily fly into blind rage. Through continued spiritual practice, your mind will become clearer and you will grasp the underlying reality of any situation. Understanding the underlying reality will enable you to show genuine heart-felt compassion for your self and others in any situation.

Compassion, a Disarming Quality

When we are in union with our own soul, we merge with the spirit of all others. At this point, we truly respect others and see them as our own brothers and sisters. This energy of deep compassion penetrates everyone and also gains the support of nature for you. The most violent, hateful people will melt in the heat of your compassionate heart.

Developing Compassion

As discussed earlier, compassion arises from the heart. Therefore, use a heartfelt approach to deepen compassion rather than an ego-centered, intellectual attitude.

Most people believe that their thoughts, words, and actions have no impact on this world. This is not true—every one of our thoughts, words, and actions ripple outward as waves of energy and affect others. Therefore, think positive thoughts. When someone is suffering and needs help, focus on that person's wellbeing and send them healing energy. Focus on your heart when you do this. Feel your heart expanding and sending warm, loving energy toward the other person.

Another exercise to help deepen your compassion is to sit in meditation with your eyes closed and visualize someone who is causing you anger or someone who is suffering. When you breathe in, visualize that you are absorbing the Life Force into your heart. When you breathe out, visualize warm, loving vibrations or rays of light moving outward and encircling the other person. Make sure that you are sincere and doing this exercise while tuned into your heart.

Over time, your *Shakti* (Life Force) becomes more potent, and you can send loving energy to heal entire families, cities and countries.

Never underestimate the power of compassionate, well-intentioned thoughts arising from your heart.

Lesson 32

Understanding and Curing Addictions

Habits and addictions are nothing but repetitive thought patterns that have etched grooves in your mind. If you repeatedly think the same obsessive thought, that thought will cut a groove in your mind and leave a deep impression which then becomes a mental habit. With more repetition, these mental habits eventually turn into obsessions and addictions. Like an old record album that has a scratch on it, when you come across a situation that triggers an old mental habit, you go back to whatever compulsions arise from these repetitive thought patterns as if the same song plays in your mind, over and over again.

This lesson will explore why we develop addictions and the effects of addictions on body, mind and spirit. It will also present tools and techniques for eliminating addictions.

Why We Develop Addictions

The reasons I cite for addictions arise from three different levels of consciousness:

> **1**-At the deepest level, we need to recognize that we give away our spiritual power to addictive substances because we are afraid of our own immense potential (godliness); we are also afraid of trusting the universe and what we were ordained to do in this lifetime. Without a trust in the universe's divine plan for us, our own divine

power may be too overwhelming to digest; so we choose to numb our Life Force through addictive substances because our own infinite potential is too overwhelming for our egos.

2-At a less profound level of consciousness, we become addicted because of our unwillingness to face deep inner pain and old wounds hidden deep in our subconscious mind. At this level, every addiction represents our unconscious refusal to face and walk through our inner pain. If we do not uncover and face our inner wounds, we will not undergo transformative change. It is impossible to experience transformational change when all of our Life Force is invested in defense systems that serve to numb out our unconscious inner-pain.

3-At an even more physical level, addictions are sometimes based on cultural influences, stress, allergies, malnutrition or imbalances in our blood sugar. Each of these requires a different strategy for overcoming the addiction. For example, in the case of nutritional imbalances a variety of herbal supplements will restore balance to the body and lower a person's craving for the addictive substance.

Effects of Addictions on Body, Mind and Spirit

Addictions gradually destroy our mind. When the mind becomes obsessed with an addictive substance or behavior, we literally "lose" our mind to that addictive substance. What actually happens to an addicted person is that she totally loses control of the mind. Of course, wherever the mind goes, *Prana,* or the Life Force, also follows. In other words, the mind controls the direction in which the Life Force flows. So, when we lose our mind to an addiction, our Life Force (*Prana*) also leaves our body and flows toward the addictive substance or behavior. Since the Life Force is the spiritual electricity that enlivens our body, when we deplete our Life Force the physical body becomes weak and eventually illness takes over.

Once we lose control over our mind and the mind begins to crumble we cannot complete and succeed in any project. Without a steady and clear mind, a person cannot accomplish anything.

Spiritually speaking, another negative effect of any addictive behavior is that we lose contact with the present moment and its requirements. Whenever we engage in an addictive pattern, our consciousness "checks out" of the present moment. When we check out though addictions, we leave the present moment, and whenever we are out of touch with the present moment we experience illusion and pain because we cannot fulfill the needs of the moment.

Tools and Techniques for Eliminating Addictions

The way to cure any addiction is to face our fears and inner pain right in this present moment. We can do this by simply witnessing the inner pain while maintaining awareness of our respiration and bodily sensations such as our heartbeat, perspiration, physical pain, etc.

Other steps toward conquering addictions include:
Admit that you are addicted

Most addicts are in denial of their addictions. The first step in the process of quitting an addiction is to sincerely face your inner self and confess, admit that you are addicted. There is no shame or judgment involved in this. We are simply letting go of our defensiveness because we cannot hide an addiction from our inner God.

Be clear that you want to give up your addiction

A very important second step is to be clear that you want to give up your addiction. If you have not made this vow to yourself no technique or diet can eliminate your addiction. Ask yourself: *Am I ready to eliminate this addiction? Am I committed to doing whatever it takes to overcome this addiction?* If you are truly not finished with your addiction, no expert can help you.

Look straight into your pain

Never try to suppress or avoid facing your addiction. Be bold and look straight into your pain. Experience and embrace pain fully; open up to your pain so it can freely flow out of you. A good way to look into your pain is by looking in the mirror while engaged in your addictive pattern. For example, look deep into your eyes while you are smoking or drinking. Your eyes are the windows to your soul and when you look deep into your eyes while smoking or drinking you will clearly see how you are betraying your inner God. During this exercise, do not judge yourself, just look deeply into your own eyes while you engage in your addictive behavior.

Make a list

List all the reasons why you want to continue your addiction. Then make a second list citing why you want to quit your addiction. On the second list, write down all the details about how lousy you feel after you feed your addiction. For example, you might list headaches, low energy, depression, shortness of breath, weight gain, low self-esteem, etc. Re-read the second list frequently.

Pray

In quitting any addiction, we need help from the Higher Powers. Ask these Higher Powers to come to your rescue the moment you are about to engage in your addictive pattern. A Higher Power can be your deceased father, Christ, Mohammed, your Soul, or even a bright star in the sky that you have loved since childhood.

Meditate

Meditation disentangles us from our thoughts and emotions and enables us to float above our mind like a peaceful witness. As a calm witness, you can observe thoughts and emotions that trigger your addictions without reacting to these thoughts and emotions.

Create a daily journal for your addiction

When you write in this journal, pour your soul and utmost sincerity onto the pages. When you engage in your addiction, journal how you felt right after engaging in your addictive behavior. Also, write in your journal which events triggered your addiction and how you felt physically and emotionally right before you engaged in your addictive ritual. Note in your journal when you are most at risk and vulnerable. Each week, re-read and analyze your diary of addiction.

Unleash the power of your soul through art

Any form of creativity and art will unleash the power of your soul. With that power you can overcome any challenge. Writing is a powerful way of tapping into your creativity. You can also take up photography, painting, poetry, dance, singing, etc. Dealing with things of beauty improves self-esteem and heals our inner pain.

Avoid defensiveness

Defensiveness is one way that we deny our addiction. Defensiveness just props up the ego. Remember, ego is that wounded part of us that craves for the addiction. By craving addiction, ego separates us from God and there is no pain greater than separation from God. We must treat the mind and ego like little children; when they are in pain, give them love and acceptance.

Find support

Support groups are very important when we are quitting addictions. Find supportive, non-judgmental people who understand your problem. Get together once a week and let each person speak while the others listen with empathy and without much comment. If you have access to a good therapist, psychotherapy can also be very useful when we are uncovering our inner pain.

Once you find a support network you might set a future date by which time you want to quit your addiction. Telling your support group friends about your target date can energize your commitment to quit your addiction.

Lesson 33

The *Guru* and Spiritual Practice (*Sadhana*)

A Guide or sage is one who has traveled the spiritual path that and that is why he can lead others down the same path. The *Guru* has personally experienced the divine potential that lies in the soul of every human being.

A Guru speaks to large audiences and also to a select number of students whom the *Guru* later takes on as disciples. Larger crowds also receive inspiration from the Guide, but a few students actually enter into an apprenticeship with the *Guru* in order to implement the *Guru's* spiritual teachings and practices into daily life.

When a *Guru* accepts a student as an apprentice, that seeker commits her life to the requirements of spiritual practice alongside the Guru. The apprentice adopts a serious and rigorous program of self-care that nourishes the mind, body and soul. What the apprentice gains is a new and more profound perspective on life that is deeper than the reality perceived through the five senses. Although spiritual awakening does not change the day-to-day events of the material world, the apprentice begins to perceive life through a new set of lenses.

The Guide's Intention

The Guide's intention is not to attract large masses of followers, rather, the intention is to stretch the student's ego and mind and inspire the apprentice to go beyond his or her own self-limiting concepts.

In training apprentices, the *Guru* works intimately to spiritually nourish each individual based on their specific needs. The true *Guru* must be very awake and present with each of the apprentices in order to understand their unique nature and needs. So, there is an intimate, one-to-one relationship between the *Guru* and each one of his apprentices must break through limiting beliefs and habits lodged in the subconscious mind in order to grow.

Spiritual Training Program (*Sadhana*)

The spiritual training program aims to nourish the student's body, mind and spirit. The goal is to raise the apprentice's overall level of consciousness.

As the apprentices' level of consciousness rises and they can handle higher voltages of spiritual energy, a *Guru* passes on more advanced techniques and deeper knowledge suitable for the advanced seekers. These techniques and more powerful spiritual energies will not be passed on until the seeker is ready, ripe, and totally receptive to the spiritual electricity of the Guru. There is no point in pressuring a *Guru* for more advanced methods as advanced techniques are only revealed once your mind, body and soul are ready to receive such techniques.

Deepening of Faith

The work of raising our consciousness and spiritual energy is indeed demanding work. What we are doing through spiritual practice is changing our biological and mental makeup.

Initially, a seeker will be attracted to the *Guru's* message and may believe that this Guide will be a knowledgeable one, but deep faith based on direct experience has not yet set in. At this stage, the seeker believes that the *Guru* and her techniques will be useful, but the seeker does not yet have certain faith that it is possible to attain the *Guru's* level of mastery over the body, mind and spirit.

Faith is different from belief; faith is stronger than belief. Belief is suspecting that spiritual knowledge and practices are beneficial. Based on belief, we initially dive into spiritual practice, hoping that we will some day establish a more permanent contact with the God Force. When we directly experience higher energies and levels of consciousness, our belief then turns into faith. With a continuation of powerful spiritual experiences, faith deepens and we finally attain spiritual certainty. Spiritual certainty means knowing that one is in communion and constantly supported by the God Force.

The decision to develop faith is a seeker's own choice. The *Guru* cannot force faith. As the seeker struggles with the issue of faith, a Guru watches lovingly and encourages the student to continue with his practices and self-healing. Sometimes when an apprentice is discouraged and fainthearted, the Guru purposely refrains from intervening. The loving intention here is let the seeker struggle and develop faith from within.

Each student's response to the spiritual training program is unique and different. This is why Guides do not encourage apprenctices to discuss and compare their experiences with one another.

All enlightened *Gurus* will tell you that the biggest obstacle blocking your self-realization is lack of self-confidence and faith in your own infinite potential. If you cannot trust our own self, doubt scatters your mental concentration and physical energy.

The Test

The God Force puts each seeker through a rigorous test to see how well that person can implement the spiritual practices in his daily life.

Many times a Guide's behavior and words are confusing and baffling to the student. This is because the *Guru* intuitively acts in such a way as to challenge the seeker's self-limiting beliefs and habitual behavior patterns. We must all understand that personal transformation and change come through the pain and effort of demolishing each of our self-defeating beliefs and behaviors.

The Practices (*Sadhana*)

No *Guru* in this world can permanently instill inner peace and clarity of mind in a seeker. It is always the seeker's responsibility to accomplish this through daily and lifelong application of spiritual principles. Only prolonged and continuous application of *sadhana* can alter your consciousness.

The *Guru* does not gather armies of followers nor does he need anyone's encouragement. Noble Guides always dodge compliments. The *Guru's* joy comes from the seeker's attainment of self-realization – the realization that we are all made in the image of god with the same infinite potential.

Lesson 34

Contemplation

Each of us goes through many experiences in life, both inner and outer experiences. Yet, few of us stop for a moment to contemplate our life experiences. Contemplation is the intuitive and emotional digestion of our life experiences. It is through the daily practice of contemplation that we receive guidance from our heart and Soul.

The reason contemplation works is that we all already know the answers to all our questions—this is called inner-knowing. Our souls have lived for hundreds, thousands of years and if we can relax our intellect and access the upper mind (*Buddhi*), we can tap into centuries of personal wisdom and experience.

Without contemplation, life passes us by and we miss the spiritual significance of many huge events. To gain wisdom, we must understand our most subtle experiences. For example, we benefit much more from each meditation if we take a moment to contemplate and understand our meditative experiences. I recommend that you keep a meditation journal at your side; in it, write down your experiences of each meditation session.

The Practice of Contemplation

The key to contemplation is relaxation of mind and body. Pose a question regarding the significance of an event, hold it in your awareness, but do not pressure yourself for an answer. Continue to contemplate your question for a few minutes each day and the answer will come when it is time. By shining the light of consciousness on any question or problem the answer suddenly appears as crystal clear insight.

Before posing your question, ask yourself if you are afraid of hearing the answer from your heart and soul. If you are not ready to listen to your inner-wisdom, and have an aversion to your own inner truth, the answers will take longer to arrive because your soul will stop speaking to you. One of the biggest obstacles to contemplation is doubt. Ask yourself, *am I willing to listen for the Soul's answers in a sincere, humble and vigilant way?* You can also pose this inner question: *If I receive sacred insight, am I willing to act on it and put it into practice?* Those who have not reached deep inner honesty will substitute an intellectual, false voice for *the still voice inside*.

Contemplate each problem and go as deep as you can following slow exhalations and emptying your mind as you exhale. A lot of people feel the intuitive answer arise from their heart. Spiritual answers are not in the form of linear logic; rather, these kinds of answers arrive in the form of symbols; dreams; coincidental daily encounters. Because the spiritual answer comes from within we never forget their sacred messages. Think about it, has anyone really learnt anything from an outside source? Sure, we study many books and listen to speakers, but that kind of knowledge is *learnt knowledge* or intellectual knowledge, not direct knowing. Learned knowledge lingers in our intellect for a while, and is forgotten with time. Direct knowledge learnt from experience is immediately understood and it transforms us permanently.

As you develop your spiritual practice of contemplation, remember, your fears are not real. Fears are just momentary impulses of energy generated by your mind. Be courageous; if you look fear straight in the eyes, fear will vanish like fog. Look for all the forces that are holding you back in life. Identify what negativities are poisoning your blood. What are the repetitive issues that keep coming back, even after months or years of meditation? Deeply contemplating such issues furthers your spiritual growth.

Five-Step Method for Contemplation

Below is a five-step method for contemplation. It works really well. Try it when you need to understand some deep rooted issues:

1. Define the question or subject of contemplation. To receive a clear answer, you must first ask a precise question.

2. When contemplating, create a sacred atmosphere. You can do contemplation in your regular place of meditation; light a candle if you wish. You can whisper a prayer to your dearest saint or guardian angels. Before you begin your contemplation, ask for the grace of the God Force (*Shakti*)— say to Her, *please help me understand this…. at a deeper, clearer level.*

3. Take a few moments to totally relax your body and empty your mind through long, slow, rhythmic, and smooth breathing in your stomach. Imagine that your mind-chatter is flowing out of your nostrils with each exhalation as you empty your mind with your out-breath.

4. Now, meditate on your question. Contemplation meditation is different from your regular meditation. During contemplation you simply quiet the mind, hold your question in your awareness, and listen deeply for an answer. Again these answers may arise in the form of symbols, images, or any other form of non- linear logic.

5. Write down all the details about your experience of contemplation in your spiritual journal or a special journal designated specifically for your contemplations. Write freely and do not edit anything that comes to your pen. After you have compiled a few contemplations, go back and look at past entries and recall any repetitive patterns.

Be patient as you develop your skill of contemplation. You will find that once the answers come, and you achieve greater clarity, forces of nature will rush in to support you in all your endeavors.

Lesson 35

Practical Application of Spiritual Principles

When a student first begins on the spiritual path of self-love and self-understanding, she is thirsty for knowledge. She dives into the ancient scriptures; studies the science of Yoga, Tai Chi, healthy breathing, and nutritional diet. At the onset, the apprentice's thirst for intellectual knowledge is deep and the most curious of meditation students are consumed for at least a few years in intellectual knowledge of the spiritual path..

While intellectual knowledge is very useful at the beginning of the path, direct experience of your soul (self) and its wisdom are what this journey is really about. At most, thirty percent of your efforts should be intellectual, while the other seventy percent of your effort should go into practical application of spiritual practices to your daily life.

This lesson will explore the practical application of spiritual principles to help you establish a deeper connection with your Soul.

Application and Action

Application and action are everything in the spiritual life. The Life Force, or God Force, is itself a creative force pulsating and buzzing within the interior of the atom. Since atoms are constantly vibrating with the Life Force and since everything in our material world is composed of atoms, the meaning of life itself is constant motion, activity, and change. Without activity and change, a vibrant life turns into depression.

Direct experience of your self requires practical application of these life lessons. Without the practical application of these spiritual principles in your daily life, spiritual practice becomes a burdensome chore and these written pages will just collect dust on your bookshelves.

The Power of Beneficial Action

Beneficial action is that which serves you and your society in the highest way. The spiritual aspirant considers it an honor to partake in life through beneficial action; the spiritual person serves God. To make great strides toward personal transformation, we need to serve and satisfy nature at three levels:

1. Our inner God (our Soul)

2. Our mind, physical body and emotions

3. All of society and humanity

Spiritually speaking, *verbs are always better than nouns*. Understand who you are, what your needs and society's needs are, then take action. Constantly review your strategies and actions; if they do not get you closer to your ultimate goals, revise them, and then continue taking action.

Whenever you are not satisfied with a situation, you have two simple choices—ou can either take action to improve your situation or you can get out of that situation altogether. There is no third alternative. Sitting idly, nagging, and complaining is not a third option.

The Power of Concentration and Attention

Attention means freeing the mind of all useless distractions and focusing it on your life's biggest priorities. Concentration focuses all your energies in a single direction and with concentrated effort, you can accomplish anything.

Remember,

Wherever your mind goes, your Life Force (Prana) follows.

When you focus your mind on what is important in your life, those aspects of your life grow and prosper. The power of concentration and attention can turn your mind into a powerful laser beam that burns through any obstacle.

Never doubt this natural principle—

Whatever you place your attention on grows and prospers.

The Importance of Silent Meditative Practice

Silent meditative practice is critical for direct experience of the Truth.

Meditate on your self, go within, and understand who you are and what you want in life. When you meditate deeply, you understand that the God Force that creates the entire universe is pulsating within you. Deep meditation is a true source of self-confidence. Once you know your self and what you want in life, place your attention on those activities that serve your mission and the welfare of society at large.

The Power of Emotions

All your thoughts and intentions have creative capability, because thoughts and intentions can influence the dance of the atom. However, your thoughts will not penetrate space, and will not influence the Creative Force within the atom unless you emotionalize your thoughts. You must place powerful emotions behind your thoughts. Think passionate thoughts, thoughts that move your heart. Emotions are like gun powder that energize your thoughts to penetrate space like a bullet.

If you want your thoughts to penetrate and influence others, you need to put some emotion behind your thoughts. The two emotions that most energize your thoughts and actions are love and faith.

The Power of Faith and Certainty

When you make a decision to accomplish something or turn one of your ideas into reality, never hesitate. Your biggest enemies, the reason why you have given up your dreams, are fear and doubt. Have an attitude of complete certainty and faith that you can meet life's challenges successfully.

Even if you lack self-confidence at this point, mechanically and with lots of self-discipline, assume an attitude of unwavering certainty. Keep your posture erect, smile, and look at the horizon while walking. Wherever you go, walk twenty five percent faster than before. With an erect posture, a smile, and your quick steps, you will be sending the subconscious mind a signal that "I am going places."

Willpower

Willpower is the power of focused intention backed by decisive action. When you add strong willpower to intense desire you will influence all natural forces to serve your goals.

Persist and refuse to allow defeat to enter your mind. Everyday exercise and strengthen your willpower through deliberate actions which are aligned with your goals. As you strengthen your willpower, you will send a powerful message to the Creative Force and to those around that you mean business and you are not willing to accept defeat. This message is incredibly powerful and actually mobilizes the Creative Force to assist you.

Sometimes, there is nothing in the present world that resembles your highest mission and the life that you wish to create—that is okay. If you persist in focusing your mind, emotions and willpower toward your wish, the God Force will actually manifest your unique creation even though that career or manifestation has never existed before.

Some people have plenty of willpower, but they use their willpower to achieve egocentric ends that are damaging to the self and to society. Such people do not seek the guidance of God or their soul in choosing a path.

Your ego may wish for one thing, but your soul knows better. Your soul has higher plans for you and does not want you to get distracted by little, meaningless desires. Do not stubbornly follow your ego's wishes; as the saying goes, *be careful what you wish for, you might just get it!*. Meditate deeply, understand what is truly good for you and society and then put your mighty willpower behind that beneficial wish.

Prayer

Having done everything you can to achieve your goal, now pray to God for assistance. When you do not believe in your prayer being answered, your prayer will lack power. If you have sincere love and faith in the God Force, your prayer will be answered.

Group Practice

Group spiritual practice always has more energy than individual practice. The combined and harmonious energy of a group has several effects:

- Any individual group member's energy increases.

- The group energy increases as more members join in.

- The group's energy benefits the entire geographic region or local where group practice is taking place.

Of course, while group activity benefits each of us individually we can only apply spiritual principles to our own life, not another person's life. Each person is responsible for quieting and stabilizing their own mind and nervous system. This is a spiritual law – just as you cannot eat and chew food for another person, you cannot force another person on to a path of personal growth. Others will only join in when they are ready and willing.

Release All Results to Your Soul (God)

The wisest people give their maximum effort to any project, then, release the results to nature and God. These people intuitively understand that the human ego and personality have no power over nature's creative forces.

The vibrational energy of our mind and ego are very low; these parts of us cannot influence the subatomic God Force vibrating at above one million cycles per second.

Your soul is the same as the Creative God Force. When undertaking any project, pray with love and faith to your soul and ask this Higher Self to mobilize natural forces to your side.

Lesson 36

Prana and the Six Bodies

The human body is made of six energy layers. The outermost and subtlest layer is your soul (inner God) and the innermost, and grossest layer is your physical body. Your Soul is the energy layer with the highest vibrational frequency (one million cycles per second and above), and your physical body is the energy layer with the lowest vibrational frequency (350 cycles per second). As you go through various energy layers, coming closer to your physical body, you lose energy as you become more solid and dense.

Sixth Layer—Soul

Your soul is the same divine energy as the God Force. If you imagine the God Force as fire and your soul as one burning stick drawn from the larger fire, just as one small flame is still the same element as the bigger fire, your soul is really of the same force as the universal God Force.

The vibrational frequency of your soul is very high. The science of physics teaches us that very high vibrating fields exhibit the following qualities: they are lightweight, radiant (emit hello-like luminosity produce heat, and are very energetic. These scientific attributes also related to high-vibrating spiritual people who have exihibited levitation, halos, *Kundalini* rising as well as strong charisma and unbelievable stamina.

Your soul, being God, is not concerned with your human desires and attachments. Your soul's only mission is to help your physical body and lower intellect understand that you are made in the image of God. Your soul will keep your body alive for as long as you are making progress toward Divine Light. When She deems that you cannot break through any more illusions and self-created limitations in this lifetime, the soul drops this body and life, taking on another body (the new you) so as to travel closer toward the Light.

Fifth Layer—Intuitive and Causal Body

Right beneath your divine energy layer (soul) is an energy layer composed of pure energy and Pure Consciousness. Your intuition or Sixth Sense arises from the causal body. The major type of spiritual electricity flowing in the causal body is electromagnetic energy because *Prana* or the Life Force is composed of electromagnetism.

Scientists have confirmed the importance of electromagnetism to our human existence through experiments that purposely deprived volunteers, sitting in special chambers, of electromagnetic energy. When scientists purposely depleted the small chamber of its electromagnetism, after a few seconds, the volunteers sitting in the special chamber become very depressed, fearful and lifeless.

The causal body is the one that radiates light or what we humans call a "halo". The colors radiating out of your causal body can vary. Your highest, most divine frequencies radiate a milky-white color. Pink colors reflect a state of love and compassion. Bluish/green colors reflect a state of wisdom, calmness and centeredness. Reds and oranges reflect lower, animalistic tendencies such as anger, aggression, lust and excitement. It should be mentioned here that the colors of the halos mentioned above are different from the specific hues surrounding the human *chakras*. Halos radiating from different body parts are in a constant state of flux depending on one's inner state at the time. Colors surrounding *chakras* are fixed and do not vary.

Fourth Layer—The Emotional Body

Your emotional body lies beneath your causal body. Every thought produces an emotion. Emotions are just *energy set in motion* by your thoughts.

Because emotions are also a form of energy, emotionally unstable people let past traumas leave deep energetic impressions on their emotional body. We carry these hurtful impressions in our emotional bodies until a Guide helps us dissolve these emotional impressions buried deep in our subconscious minds.

The best way to dissolve past emotional impressions is to witness them and yet fully feel them, without being entangled with such emotions. Identification with passing emotions destabilizes this energy field and causes disease. Emotions are impermanent; the best way to deal with difficult emotions is to follow your inhalations and exhalations while reciting the mantra, "this too shall soon pass."

Third Layer— The Mental Body

This energy layer is where your subconscious mind and lower mind (intellect) reside. The sense of "I" or ego also comes from the mental body. The mind and ego are twins; whenever you have thoughts, the sense of "I" or ego is born.

The subconscious mind is the storage house of all your past thoughts, emotions, and memories. All your mental concepts, conclusions, and opinions come from the subconscious mind.

All your past thoughts are stored in the mental layer as footprints or impressions. Know that a thought is energy and every bit of energy leaves an impression or footprint on your mental layer. The mental body also carries all memories from your past lives. Past-life memories are stored and hidden in your subconscious mind. Past-life memories can be brought forth into consciousness through deep hypnosis and sometimes deep relaxation.

Every one of your thoughts affects your physical body through your nervous system and special amino acids that your body secretes in reaction to each thought. These amino acids are called neuropeptides. Your thoughts, therefore, create bio-chemical reactions that affect your body cells.

As we have discussed in previous lessons, in most people, rather than the Soul being in charge, the mind and its constant chatter are in command. When your mind is in command, you experience pain. In the case of enlightened people, the mental layer is continuously receiving the light of the soul. Allow your mind to be the servant of your soul, not the other way around.

Second Layer — Vital Body

This energy layer is composed of pure *Prana* or Life Force. This energy layer collects and distributes *Prana* by way of your *chakras* and *nadis*.

All movement of the Life Force is made possible by the Vital Body. Your Life Force is a gold colored beam of light that flows through your nerves and subatomic energy channels called *nadis*. Without this flow, you would be dead in a second. Just as blood flows through your veins, *Prana* flows through your nervous system and your *nadis*, keeping your body alive.

Your six *chakras* (major energy centers) and your 72,000 *nadis* (subatomic conduits of *Prana)* are part of your Vital Body. A vital and successful life in the material world means balanced energy management and energy distribution throughout your body. With meditation, you become aware of your inner energy—where you are losing energy, and where in life you are gaining energy. With that kind of awareness, you can choose to participate in activities that increase your *Prana*. With heightened awareness, you will naturally dodge people and situations that deplete your energy.

The well adjusted person can direct *Prana* up and down the spinal column through any and all of the *chakras*. As our awareness and consciousness rises toward God Consciousness, our higher *chakras* become more radiant and active.

First Layer — Physical Body

This energy layer is the densest and slowest moving layer, vibrating at 350 cycles per second. The physical layer forms our visible body with all of its internal organs. Although the physical body seems solid, inside each cell and atom is is mostly emptiness.

Before we experience any illness in our physical body, one of the finer energy layers described above will have fallen out of balance. An imbalance in the subtle Life Force always precedes physical illness. Energy healers specialize in healing the finer, more subtle energy layers in order to heal the physical body.

Lesson 37

Going Beyond Our Limited Beliefs

The science of enlightenment teaches that the mind cannot see beyond the walls of the mind. At the intellectual and thinking levels the mind is conditioned by our past experiences and will not accept new realities. The conditioned mind which is not managed through mindfulness or awareness, will keep superimposing its memories of past experiences on the present moment.

In order to experience enlightenment, we must symbolically burst open our skulls and solicit the help of a Guru who can show us how to melt-down our own self-limiting beliefs.

Release all your core beliefs about what is right or wrong. To do this, you must relax into nothingness, allowing your repetitive thoughts and beliefs to dissolve into the *Ujjayi* breath. Listen deeply to the sound of *Ujjayi* breath and soon you will be aware that you have no thoughts, no beliefs, no body, no ego. In this vast space of relaxed awareness you are open to millions of new realities that naturally come to you in the freshness of the moment. You see in Yoga, we do not change the world, we simply change the color of the lenses through which you perceive the world.

When we release all our rigid and conditioned beliefs, life suddenly opens up and many of our wishes manifest, as if effortlessly. In such moments of receptivity and harmony with the God Force, it all seems effortless because we are not fighting our natural self and we are not resisting the laws of nature.

Three Limiting Beliefs that Hold Us Back

There are three core negative beliefs of the mind which most people suffer from; these are called *malas* in Sanskrit, which they keep us from experiencing our unbounded potential:

1. *The Feeling of Unworthiness and Limitation*

This is the *original sin*. The internal message is *I am not good enough just as I am now*, and the emotion is typically one of deep shame about who we are. Ultimately, the sense of shame comes from low self-esteem; and low self-esteem itself comes from not having seen a wonderful reflection of ourselves in the mirror of our parents' eyes when we were very young (up to the age of five) In a more spiritual sense, this feeling that "I am not good enough", comes from lack of awareness that we are gods—that the God Force is a divine energy vibrating outside and within our bodies. Most people's minds have been conditioned for years to think that somehow they are not worthy and capable of infinite progress. This is because they are ignorant of their own divine potential.

2. *The Feeling of Separation and Multiplicity*

This feeling arises from the individual ego and the sense that *I am separate and different from all else.* As long as we identify with our individual ego and physical body, we feel lonely and vulnerable in such a big world, because we feel ultimately feel separate from the One God Force that pulsates within all of us. Many negative emotions such as arrogance, conceit and judgment arise from the ego's separatist tendencies.

As our meditation deepens and we directly experience inner joy and communion with the Soul, our sense of loneliness and separation from *the whole* begins to vanish. It feels as if there is some One watching and accompanying us through all the days of our lives. This some One is actually The Witness of Pure Consciousness which is silent awareness that follows us around even in the midst of activity.

When we learn to love our own Self, we also begin to be aware of other people's souls instead of their outer appearance and personalities. When we love someone's soul, we love them unconditionally and permanently. Daily changes in appearance, mood, and personality do not lessen our love for others.

3. *The Sense of Personal Control and Doer-ship*

Ego-centered people believe that they are or should be in complete charge of daily life events. Such individuals cannot feel good about themselves until they accomplish things with perfection; the dysfunction of perfectionism actually arises from fear of losing control. Perfectionists need to earn love and recognition by always "doing" and through external accomplishments instead of just "being" perfect and acceptable just as they are.

In such cases, one's sense of self-love is conditioned by external success or accomplishment. Your individual ego may feel so threatened that you may go through years of struggle and hardship until some external authority figure affirms, *now you are okay; now you are allowed to love yourself.*

An enlightened person develops such a deep internal sense of unconditional self-love that they intrinsically understand that *I am lovable just in my natural state of Being; I do not necessarily need to do anything to become lovable.*

In terms of who is ultimately in control of human life, classic Yogic philosophy believes that you as a physical body and social personality, do nothing—it is actually Soul-Power, or that spiritual electricity that animates you, which is the Doer. The enlightened person understands that her soul (sixth energy layer) is the Doer. The Soul or personal God is the same creative energy that manifests all external objects and events. The enlightened person places maximum energy in any worthy project, then releases the actual results of any effort to God. This kind of person has no obsession about controlling the outer events of his life. Here, we are talking about someone who participates fully in life, someone who takes action, but knows when and how to release control and not be totally consumed by the results.

I will conclude this lesson by reiterating that the conditioned mind programmed and set in its own core beliefs must be catapulted into unknown and new dimensions through a literal meltdown of its old framework. This is what the Guru does for the apprentice. There is literally life before you met your Guide and life after you meet your Guru. If your Guide is a realized One, you can distinctly recognize that point in your life when everything began to change for the better because your Guide helped you change the color of the lenses through which you experience and perceive life (your beliefs).

Completion—Coming Full Circle

Dear Friend,

You may have had a direct experience of your Soul—that vast field of silence that lies behind the ego and mind. You may have found new confidence, just making momentary contact with this inner silence.

The knowledge of the Soul is both the source and the end of all knowledge; but as you would have discovered, you cannot grasp the vastness and richness of the soul through your intellect and five senses. Never try, since your mind and ego arise from your soul they cannot begin to grasp their own Source.

Though I have tried to share my experience of connecting with the Soul in the introduction of this book, the experience of nothingness or direct contact with the Soul is really beyond words and explanations. The only way to contact the Soul is for your ego and mind to dissolve into the experience of meditation. I liken this experience to a wave slipping back into the ocean and vanishing into its Source. As long as there is an "I" or some person trying to meditate, your meditation will not be deep and will seem like a burdensome exercise that you try to avoid. As soon as you surrender your ego and mind to each exhalation and let yourself dissolve into the breath, you will experience the vast expanse of your soul with all of its knowledge.

Proceed cautiously along your spiritual path. There are many pitfalls as there are many Guides who do not have worthy intentions. Be alert and access your inner wisdom. Never submit your sense of integrity to any teacher until you can directly verify some of your Guide's advice through direct exerience. Do not blindly follow your Guide or others; seek enlightenment for yourself. Your true *Guru's* greatest satisfaction will be to see you become a realized and inner-directed soul.

Find out what you want in life, seek the perfection of your soul, practice your meditation at every opportunity, continue to develop one-pointed concentration and concentrate on the skill of merging with your meditation the same way that a wave leaves the shore and slides back into the sea. Do not stop until your mind and nervous system naturally learn to release and dissolve into the vast silence of your inner depths. The journey may seem long at times, but your persistence and patience will pay off.

Do not get involved in controversial conversations. The more inner joy you feel, the more inwardly confident you will become—no need to engage in so many debates. Know you own Truth and follow it, all the while stepping lightly on this Earth. You will see no point in proving yourself or your views to others. Guard your inner silence and joy. Remember, your main relationship is between you and your inner God. Keep the company of loving and wise friends and let go of your attachment to destructive habits and friends who rob you of your hope and aspirations.

Whenever you can, all day long if possible, whisper the name of God, whatever word or image comes to you. Whispering or chanting the name of God has a powerful healing effect on the mind and nervous system. Whatever inner-image or positive self-talk that you repeat hundreds of times, etches a groove in your mind. If these images and words are loving and empowering, you will literally be placing yourself into a bliss and empowering trance through such mental and verbal repetitions. By doing this practice, your ego will bathe under the light of your soul—try it.